BRITISH & AMERICAN
GAME-BIRDS

BRITISH & AMERICAN GAME-BIRDS

By H. B. C. Pollard *and* Phyllis Barclay-Smith

With a chapter on shooting in America by
Eugene V. Connett III

Illustrated by
Philip Rickman

THE DERRYDALE PRESS
LANHAM AND NEW YORK

THE DERRYDALE PRESS

Published in the United States of America
by The Derrydale Press
4720 Boston Way, Lanham, Maryland 20706

Distributed by NATIONAL BOOK NETWORK, INC.

Original Derrydale printing 1993
First paperback printing with french folds 1999

CONTENTS

v

LIST OF ILLUSTRATIONS

INTRODUCTION

I T is one of the signs and portents of our times that the future of many species of ducks should be less dependent on their fate at the hands of nature than at the hands of man. Nevertheless, during the last twenty years man has become increasingly aware of the need for preservation and conservation. In Europe the decrease of wildfowl became threatening and the International Committee for Bird Preservation came into being. It is under the presidency of Monsieur Delacour and it is fully representative of the leading European nations. Its efficiency depends on the promotion and implementing of suitable legislation by the Sections representative of their countries.

The International Committee and their sectional sub-committees are typical of the new thought, the broader and perhaps more democratic thought of to-day. The representative members include a large number of practical sportsmen and it is not a question of spurious sentimentalism, such as has too often defeated practical measures in the past, but of a sound working alliance between the widest possible interests affected. The British sub-committee dealing with the Protection of Wildfowl was successful in obtaining a month's extra close season for ducks and geese. This was not a victory imposed on a reluctant body of sportsmen: it was a matter of perfect agreement between the sportsmen, who represented their organisations, wildfowlers, gamekeepers, ornithologists and eminent naturalists were all on the panel. The commercial interests who breed duck and the far larger ones who sell them, were all in agreement. Every point, and perhaps a good deal that was wide of the point, was hammered out, and the result was an effective simple Bill which gave an additional month's close time and prohibited the import of duck killed abroad during the English close season.

In general, it is considered that the effect of sportsmen shooting fairly, does not represent any very serious toll of the multitude of wildfowl. The commercial exploitation of wildfowl as food is, however, a very serious matter. It is judged that the duck decoys in Holland and in the Baltic countries kill an immeasurably greater number of duck than all the sportsmen in Europe.

In the further north, the nesting duck are destroyed and the eggs represent a commodity. It is not possible to say at this date quite how this matter can be dealt with, but it is to be hoped that legislation prohibiting all imports of this type will be implemented in the more advanced countries of Europe and America.

There is, however, a slight counterpoise to this depletion of ducks. If you have a lake, or even a good sized pond, it is much easier to breed wildfowl than is usually realised, and it is not a hobby which need clash with your demand for shooting. I do not suppose that any ornamental water is without its brilliant little Carolina teal, yet twenty-five years or so ago, eminent ornithologists were saying that they would follow the dodo and the passenger pigeon. To-day I should think that the Carolina teal is as plentiful in its protected state as any bird.

You may say that it is ridiculous to bring up ducks, rare or common, on private water, but it is not. It means an effective reserve of something which might otherwise be lost for ever. I believe that all bison in Canada and in the National Park of the U.S.A. were bred from European zoological specimens.

Practically speaking, the march of time which involves the intensive development of any country for the human race, must restrict the food area of its fauna. Marshes are drained: bricks and mortar restrict the country, and where forty years ago there was wild game, no wire fences and very little disturbance, to-day those conditions have gone.

It is no good crying about it. The job of the present generation is to see that we stabilise affairs before they go too far. Game-birds are beginning to be internationalized. In every country some species have dwindled nearly to extinction, and we now know that the cause is not so much "the man with the gun" as the man with the bricks and mortar and concrete, or the mechanical tractor.

Nothing can be finer than the way in which the pheasant is doing his best to replace indigenous game in the United States. They have to meet the competitive interests of native-born predatory animals, and one of the troubles of the acclimatisation of game birds is that they bring their own parasitic diseases with them. Some race of birds which has developed a considerable resistance factor to its own diseases may introduce some novel strain to indigenous birds, and, so far as is possible, introduction should be scientifically supervised.

There are only a handful of naturalists who are familiar with game-bird diseases and who have practical experience as game raisers. It is not difficult for any competent scientific worker who can use a compound microscope and has access to a suitable library, to identify by name ninety per cent of the parasites we meet in game-birds and ducks. Yet these parasites are responsible for more than half the mortality, probably nearer three-quarters. Remedial measures are almost unknown, for in practice what one can carry out to a moderate degree on a game farm is impossible under natural conditions.

Nutritional needs are in little better state, but year by year we are gaining greater knowledge. That which appears to be an insoluble problem to-day may crack up any time in the next decade. I do not believe that the future will see a sterile, gameless, world, but I think that wise legislation, backed up by public opinion, and, above all, by the sportsman's innate sense of fairness, will preserve for our children sufficient to shoot, and I feel that quality will be wanted more than quantity.

H. B. C. POLLARD

Wisboro Green, Sussex
June, 1939

GROUSE AND BLACK GAME

THE most expensive game-bird in Europe is the Red Grouse—and it is expensive because it is very, very limited to certain specially favoured areas and it is a bird of incomparable gastronomic value. There is no flavour in the world even moderately comparable to that of grouse, just as nothing really approaches perfect caviare! Also it affords the best of all sporting shooting in the world. It is possible that the range of grouse could be extended, but a few facts have to be considered first. The Red Grouse (*Lagopus scoticus*) is a bird dependent on a particular environment and a specific food plant. That plant is the heather, and in the north of England and Scotland heather takes seven years to grow to more than knee-high. In the Mediterranean, especially in Corsica, the same little shrub grows more than man-high in quick time, and the ordinary pipe smoker with his "briar" pipe is smoking a red root of close-textured heather. Briar is simply the trade name for "bruyere" or heather—an anglicised version.

Now in favourable surroundings heather grows to a more than man-high scrub or "maquis," but inscrutable wisdom keeps the grouse bird to its normal height, and grouse cannot feed on heather that grows like Jack and the Beanstalk.

It might be practicable if we could cross grouse with ostriches or cassowaries, but there again—we can't!

The Red Grouse can stand a heavy snowfall and lives in tunnels under the snow, but grouse are thirsty birds and need peat-water. Below the snow at ground-level unfrozen water is available. But grouse will not thrive or continue in a country where the surface water and the top spit of the earth are frozen hard before the snow blanket sets in and allows the heat of the earth to thaw it out below the snow surface. Therefore, attempts to acclimatise grouse in very cold countries have failed even if the heather environment seemed good. Because of the different growth rate and height of the heather, attempts to introduce them in hot countries have failed.

It is necessary for the Red Grouse (though less necessary for the Black Cock) that the bird should have heather for food and a predominantly acid water environment, plus quartz grit to grind up the heather in the gizzard.

The biggest of the grouse tribe, the Capercaillie, is a tree bird, but he gets an equivalent effect from his food which is mainly the very astringent and resinous points of conifers. It may seem unnecessarily wide to speak of grouse as needing an *acid* environment, but it is ecologically sound. Heather is a shrub of acid environment in terms of soil acidity, and the internal canal of the grouse is several points of pH more acid than that of any other game-bird.

You can hatch grouse eggs and rear the brood on a very wide variety of food—but it will be found that "grouse chicks prefer peat-water above all other water." This is not odd, but so far as I can see facts, is simply because grouse interiors have to have suitably acid (probably humic and tannic vegetable acids) bias. If we do not give them this acid bias— the strongyle worms or coccidiosis (a protozoan infection) and possible bacterial invasion get the upper hand and the grouselets perish!

The only hope that I can see of acclimatising Red Grouse is to find a place where the ground is acid, hilly, and peaty, and with adequate heather and quartz grit and the extremes of temperature not too severe. Parts of northern Portugal would seem to answer this prescription, but there the heather grows too fast and out of reach. You cannot acclimatise grouse there, although every condition seems right, simply because heather grows out of feeding-reach and is not adequate in quantity. With regular annual burning, I think it might be done. One might perhaps get a quantity of grouse acclimatised, by hand rearing, but I doubt they would take hold and increase as wild birds. The odds are against it. In fact we are not in the least likely to improve on Nature's provisions in Europe with European birds. We humans can't beat Nature's thousands of years of environment. But when it comes to a new continent like the United States of North America, then if we took a geological map and made a very careful study of the meteorological conditions there might be a few places which would carry heather and once heather was acclimatised—could carry grouse.

It is, I admit, not a very practical suggestion from an economic point of view, but it is the only possible way of transplanting this particular bird to a new continent, and it is far better to look along these lines than to consider vague introductions (always an expensive and foredoomed business) if the conditions are not right.

The points to be considered are the grouse's alimentary canal. True heather, acid peat-water, a not too severe winter, quartz grit to grind up the food, and even if we find all these things—no hostile vermin capable of beating the experiment.

I doubt that these conditions exist—but you know they might! Black Game demands less exigent conditions. They too need an acid environment, but to a lesser degree, and they thrive on the edges of moor and cultivation. They can do well on some mainly sandy soils of heath where the conditions favour ling (which is called heather, but is not the real Scotch heather) and they can live in the surroundings of the ling, bilberry, and rough scrub of the New Forest. Introductions in East Anglia failed after a few years and they are sparsely established on Exmoor where conditions are more acid. Broadly speaking they do not thrive on light land of the true sand waste type, but where there are sufficient peat-bogs or waters of high acid concentration and the vegetation is ling, cranberry, and whortle, they can exist. Even in Scotland they do not always make headway, and their disappearance in England is probably more due to improved methods of cultivation and the drainage of land in the early nineteenth century than to any other cause we can discern. If we consider them as a bird whose natural habitat is just beyond the confines of cultivation and on predominantly acid moors and sheep walks, but which comes down to the edge of the cultivated ground far more than do Red Grouse, we get a generalised view of the surroundings in which they can thrive.

The food list of the black cock and grey hen—known as Black Grouse [*Lyrurus tetrix* (L)]; *Tetrao tetrix* (L)] or to sportsmen as Black Game, is wide. The French name, Coq de Bruyere specifies its natural environment. In Germany it is known as the Auerhahn. It lives on heather or ling tops, whortleberry shoots and fruits, cranberries, and blueberries, the fruit of the rowan or mountain ash, shoots of larch and coniferous trees, birch buds and a variety of grass and sedges. The feed of the young is largely insects, and in the early autumn they feed greedily on the stubbles and shoots of oats and corn in the cultivations adjoining the moorlands.

It is not difficult to see from this that the food intake is consistent with an acid environment, particularly in the first few weeks of life.

Its Continental stretch is fairly wide, and it thrives where the Red Grouse which needs a far higher degree of acidic environment has never been able to be established. It stretches north up to 68 degrees across Scandinavia and Russia. Its southern limit is about 51 degrees and though familiar in Austria and the Carpathians, it does not extend to the Pyrenees. In Asia east of the Altai and Urals associated forms occur right through the mountain country of Manchuria. Some of these, of which little is known, might possibly adapt better in the United States. There is a far wider possibility of the extension of the range of Black Game to some sections of the United States where suitable regional conditions may be available than is the case with the red grouse. As the Black Cock's feathers figure proudly in the Scotch bonnet it is to be hoped that the Scotch in North America will consider the question of introduction into glens in foothill environment where geological and climatic conditions seem suitable. I had a discussion with a native-born Scotch mining engineer who had prospected widely in the States. He was of the opinion that some sections of the Appalachians would suit both grouse and Black Game. I doubt the expediency of trying Red Grouse till Black Game have shown their possibility of acclimatisation.

Introductions in the North Temperate Zone are always potentially feasible, provided the ecological environment is right. In the Southern hemisphere, Temperate Zone birds do not always realise that our Christmas is midsummer "down there," and the Australian Black Swan, though long introduced and bred in England, will produce eggs at a wholly inadvisable time of year. In fact just when we are getting our skates ground!

The difficulties of introducing Red Grouse to the American continent are complicated by their meteorology. The climate of Great Britain has a poor reputation among pleasure seekers and sun worshippers, but against that it must be remembered that it seldom proceeds to extremes. We may not hunt because of an iron frost holding us up for a week or ten days—while in the States hounds have to meet under conditions of frost which appal a visitor. Here snow lies most of the winter on the higher hills and mountains, but brooks run, the earth with its heat-losses from radiation conserved by the snow is relatively warm and grouse burrow and feed under the snow. Black Game are not quite so good at this. Abel Chapman described how he found the Red Grouse economically efficient under the heavy snow pall of the English-Scottish border, but the Black Game less able to find sustenance when Nature's iron grip closed down. If one looks into the question of how the Red Grouse have survived as a distinct species in the United Kingdom, it must on the whole be due to regional distribution in an ecological environment which is suitable, but where meteorological differences are not those which prevail on the continental zones. The swiftly changing weather of Great Britain, the equable flow of the warm Gulf Stream currents make our islands a very different place to the grim, long, hard winters of the frozen continents.

Conditions of climate hard enough to provoke a seven years' growth of heather before it attains maturity at a height of eighteen inches to two feet appear to control the feed conditions of the grouse species, where heather grows to a man-high shrub under advanced temperate or semi-tropical conditions mechanical conditions put food out of reach of the birds. There does not appear to me to be at the moment any other interpretation, but if these generalisations are taken into consideration, it might be possible to find foci where introduction was possible and spread might occur. But I do not think that a seeming similarity with ecological conditions is sufficient to warrant any attempt at introduction or hope of acclimatisation. An exact parallel must be sought. It would be a blessing to sportsmen—and perhaps a loss to Scotland—if the grouse species were ever successfully introduced. I do not think that in the present state of knowledge success is very probable, but it is always possible. Some place which is now a sheep-run half-way to Patagonia and Cape Horn might conceivably be the best natural grouse country in the world.

The white grouse or Ptarmigan is a bird of high altitudes. It too may present possibilities if the food plants are analogous, but there is really so little known about the food or the ecological environment of the grouse family that it would take an expert—and there are only about three of these in the world, to decide whether there was any hope of success in transplanting this species. And it would take him over a year to examine conditions and make up his mind.

On the other hand it is better to pay heavily for a real sound and scientific report than to waste money on a foredoomed project which cannot be called an experiment.

There may be favoured spots where the Red Grouse will thrive, but so far as knowledge goes at present, there is nothing outside the islands of the United Kingdom.

The Ruffed Grouse of America, *Bonasa umbellus*, called Partridge or Birch Partridge in the north and Pheasant in some of the States farther south, like the Capercaillie, is a tree bird. Though it likes hilly country, it affects dim forests and deep thickets. It appears to be dependent on trees and does not like open plains, for where woods are destroyed it soon disappears. It is probably hardier than the British grouse, for it is able to stand up to extremely cold weather. Though a popular and well-known game-bird, comparatively little has been written of its habits, for where it is much shot it is very shy and wary. Observers who have found the bird in places where it is left in peace state that it is there very different in character, with little fear of man.

The loud drumming which it makes with its wings, and which can be heard almost a mile off, is a familiar sound in the woods, but the actual performance has not frequently been witnessed. The thunderous whirr of wings it so often makes when rising from the ground is no doubt a protective "aggression" to confound the approaching enemy, for it can fly and alight as quietly as most birds.

GROUSE: A DIAGRAM OF VARIETIES

Black form, ♂ and ♀.   White form, ♂ and ♀

August, ♂ and ♀.

Red form, ♂ and ♀.   Buff-spotted form, ♀, near bird.
                             Buff barred form, ♀, second bird.

The Ruffed Grouse has a very varied diet, partly insectivorous, but largely vegetable. It is particularly addicted to fruit and will eat cultivated apples, plums, and cherries in addition to wild grapes and all sorts of berries. It also eats the berries of the poison sumac and poison ivy with impunity, and, unfortunately, during the late autumn, will take the leaves of alder, which makes its flesh very bitter, and quite poisonous to some people.

PARTRIDGES: SPRING IN THE SOUTH DOWNS

PARTRIDGES AND QUAIL

THE partridge family, as it is recognised by sportsmen, groups into three distinct branches—the true Partridge, *Perdix perdix*, the French partridge, *Alectoris rufa*, or *Caccabis rufa*, to use an older classification much easier to follow, and the Quail, *Coturnix communis*. Nearly all the partridges of hot countries are variations of the French partridge, which have different plumage or habits and are so dignified as sub-species, but the Himalayan Chukor, the Barbary partridge, the Spanish partridge, and many other species are simply very slightly different editions of our old friend *Caccabis rufa*. All those species can interbreed and it is possible that by the selection of special species for special environments more can be done for acclimatisation of game stocks than by a purely unselective importation of "partridges." Unfortunately the partridge family as a whole do not lay well in captivity because they are shy and diffident about mating. Success has been attained, but you can never regularly depend on it, though it is possible that a clearer understanding of dietary problems might provide the clue to a greater glandular response. Most partridges, however, can be transported alive and acclimatise successfully, but will only breed under wild or semi-wild conditions. Every year, though, game farmers report some improvement in the solution of the problem, and though they are never likely to be such beautifully plastic material as the pheasants, it is worth everyone's while to support any serious avicultural research, for if the partridge family can be as widely distributed as the pheasant family, they will thrive in agricultural areas and drier areas than are suited to the pheasant.

Rather unsuccessful introductions have been made in the past, and it is possible that it has not always been realised that what a European calls "corn" is wheat, barley, oats, or rye, and is a small grain which can be swallowed, while American "corn" is the maize which is not in its larger sizes suitable for partridge. Actually the best food for partridge is insects while young and after that clover or alfalfa. They feed in the main on the undergrowth below the cereal crops, and all the grain they take is that dropping from the ears during the harvesting. For this they scour the stubbles. In general, the birds are wholly beneficial to agriculture as the vast bulk of their food consists of vegetable matter, mainly weed and weed seeds, and a proportion (now known to be far less than was once believed) of insect life, most of which are insects injurious to agriculture.

There is not a very great deal known about the food habits of the *Caccabis* group and their arid country relatives. They are believed to be rather more insectivorous than either the true partridge or the French partridge, whose diet in the temperate climate of France and England approximates to that of the true *Perdix*. It seems probable that this is so,

7

for in really arid countries there is hardly enough vegetation to support life—yet there must be a considerable amount of seed, for when rain falls vegetation springs up in the most astounding way. On the other hand it must not be overlooked that in parts of Northern Africa which are commonly regarded as desert, two (and on occasion three) crops of barley may be grown and harvested in a year, and that the *Caccabis* group are not true desert birds like Sand Grouse, but birds able to stand an environment whose aridity is seasonal, but a very intensive florescence and harvest occurs at the right season.

One would think that to-day everything that could be known about those most common European game-birds the Grey partridge and the French partridge would be known, but it is by no means so. It is not easy to correct inaccurate statements which have received wide credence yet have been proved baseless within recent years. Most modern books have faithfully reported the findings officially given by one of the first pioneers of crop-content analysis. These gave the partridge a curiously high value of insect-life intake. I have often worked out the crop of an adult partridge and made a microscopical survey—but these were always cases of wasted, "found dead," or pathological birds sent in for examination. I must have eaten thousands of delightful partridges, but I never investigated them. Dissection is, I must admit, not conducive to appetite when it concerns the subject! Partridges in England have been suffering from a strongyle worm disease akin to the strongylosis of grouse. It is a parasitic contagious affair, for the eggs of the worms are evacuated in the droppings, hatch into larvae on the ground and climb up wet grass and vegetation to dewdrops at the tips. Partridge chicks drink these dewdrops in preference to any water, and so the cycle of infection is carried on.

In practice it is a disease of overcrowding. There has been rather a boom in English shooting because it is convenient to the business man to motor anything up to a hundred miles for his day's shooting. It is a little difficult for the business mind to rise above figures, and quantity was the standard of comparison easiest understood. Money was not particularly valued, but the economy of Nature is very different. It was no good trying to grow a pair of birds to every four acres of ground if Nature decreed that one pair to twelve acres was her limit for that kind of ground. Well, the greedy worked "intensive" systems, brought in Hungarian stock or eggs, and crowded the ground. This offended the sanitary laws for healthy partridges and the stock was not only decimated, but the opposite of decimated, if there is such a word. It was not one in ten that died, but one in ten that survived! A few lean seasons have cleared the ground, but it takes about three years to clean unless you get an autumn singularly favourable for mushroom and fungus growth, for fungi and moulds are the best cleaners-up of dangerous materials in the way of worm eggs, larvae, and protozoan oocysts. A hot, dry summer may desiccate them, but a moist, damp autumn with abundant fungoid growth is the only thing I know which really cleans ground. I like to see a fuzz of mould on bird and animal droppings on an autumn morning, for it means that these fungi have penetrated every living worm egg or infective agent of the larger parasites.

Overcrowding would again produce the same effect, and just as the cycle of grouse disease is in Scotland the sequel to the building up of a stock too great for the available food on the moor—a matter of an irregular seven years' cycle—so partridge disease is quite

the same in its general relationship. It is a disease which was in existence in pre-War days, but it was not widespread. The moment the greedy shooting folk overcrowded their land it became epizootic and spread far and wide from the responsible foci. It is not likely to affect birds introduced in a wide area in any other country, but it might give trouble in a game farm where birds were run under semi-wild, but overcrowded conditions. The disease is specific to the partridge and does not affect other birds, nor, although opinion is undecided on this point, does it affect the French partridge. There are, however, other brands of strongyle worms specific to the species of the *Caccabis* and presumably a specific form of parasitic disease will follow any attempt to overcrowd any kind of partridge in excess of the available food-supply. In the case of grouse disease we know that the acid peat-water and the acid heather diet are vital to health, but we are not certain what essential food factors besides simple nutrition are necessary to maintain the partridge in health. It is probable that acid plants like wild sorrel play an important part in the health balance of the diet, but very little is known of the special qualities of the enormous range of weeds eaten by the bird. Some of these must play an important part in keeping normal parasitic affection within non-lethal bounds, yet we still do not know for certain what these indispensable factors are.

It is by no means easy to tell the sex of partridges and quite impossible to do so while they are in flight. In the old days the Grey partridge with a horseshoe mark on his breast was deemed to be the male, but this marking is no indication of sex at all. It is, however, a very old belief, and a biological ignorance induced the older Christian writers to speak of the partridge as a lecherous and sexually perverted bird!

There are two tests which can be applied to birds in their second season, but I do not consider them absolutely certain even then, and they are very misleading if applied to young birds.

The first is that the crown of the male is plain chestnut-brown with very narrow, paler shaft stripes, while the head colour of the female seems slightly lighter because the female feathers have a larger shaft stripe. The second is easier. In the female the shoulder feathers are barred with wide stripes across a black feather while in the male there are no crossbars.

Actually, birds are found whose plumage has no relation whatever to these and any other sex-determination suggestion. Hens which have been perhaps pricked with a shot affecting the ovaries may develop male plumage and vice versa. There is no scientific way of establishing the sex except by dissection of the organs.

The Red-legged or French partridges have no sex differences in plumage, but the cock birds carry a small, flat-topped, rudimentary spur base. In the Mountain partridge or "Bartavelle," *C. saxatilis,* this base is rather more pronounced and age can be determined to some extent from its degree. The only real difference between the ordinary Red-leg and the Bartavelle is that the latter has a predominantly light grey rather than reddish dun colour and a clearer, narrower, black neck ring. The breast is also clear grey with black. The whole series of Red-legged partridges are prone to local forms which may be classed as sub-species such as the black-headed Arabian partridge (*C. melanocephala*), the Barbary partridge (*C. petrosa*), the Chukor (*C. chukar*) of the Middle East and Himalayas.

2

But when we compare the Red-leg with the common Grey partridge we have to meet a very important difference in their habits of self-preservation. The Grey partridge when alarmed squats then flashes in a covey like Quail and heads on the wing for the nearest patch of cover. The Red-leg and all his brethren do not flush on the wing, but run for about a quarter of a mile. They then squat and will flush on the wing if disturbed. This habit does not matter in a country like Great Britain where birds are almost invariably driven by beaters over the line of guns, but it would make a great deal of difference in a country where birds are for the most part still walked up over bird dogs, and it would be as well if this very distinct difference in sporting behaviour was fully recognised before Red-legged were favoured in preference to Grey partridges. The common Grey partridge is not infrequently alluded to as the Hungarian partridge. This simply because the eggs and live birds are exported from Hungary. The bird is identical with the English partridge, but in Great Britain no reputable game farm supplies or deals in English partridge eggs. In the past when there was traffic in these eggs it led to grave scandals, for as it is almost impossible to breed these birds successfully in captivity, the eggs were collected from wild nests and were obviously stolen from somebody or other's ground.

The common partridge is essentially a bird for light arable land; it never does well on heavy, water-retaining clays and is at its best on sandy soil or light soil such as gravel over chalk. The best common partridge country is plains or undulating hill country and it requires no tree covert for roosting, and nests for preference in a hedgerow or low thickets. The Red-leg is perhaps a better bird for real foothill country and true mountain surroundings and has a tendency to nest in a relatively higher position, such as tree-stumps or on the steps of haystacks, and it is, I think, less nervous of humans during incubation. A certain amount of mystery still surrounds the nesting habits of the Red-leg. In some cases the hen lays two nests and the cock bird incubates one or other of them. This habit is well defined with the Chukor, but apparently variable with the French partridge; it now seems, however, to be fully substantiated as occurring occasionally.

In general the habits and food of the Grey and Red-legged partridges are closely similar. The period of incubation for the Red-leg is in Great Britain twenty-three days, which is a day shorter than the Grey, but in an incubator a clutch may take up to twenty-five days to come off. Laying begins early in May, and fifteen eggs are about an average clutch. The eggs are buff and brown speckled and the shell is considerably harder than that of the ordinary Grey partridge. It is, however, of a rather more porous texture, and the egg is larger. It is always unwise to mix the eggs of the Grey and the Red-leg as the incubation period is different. So far as I know, there is no real hybrid between the common partridge and the Red-leg. The young of the latter when changing their first plumage sometimes look very like a cross between the two birds, but actually no case of interbreeding is known. It would take a very great deal to convince me that any true hybrid has been recorded, for I have never seen the slightest interest displayed by one species in the other, and I do not think that an unpaired Red-leg will adopt a brood of ordinary partridges, though the unpaired Grey partridge will adopt an unmothered brood of his own species.

I have not been able to find an authentic instance of a brood of Red-legs being adopted by an ordinary Grey partridge or vice versa. I have known cases where Red-leg chicks which have been hatched in an ordinary nest with the others have shared the common life of the mixed brood, but I do not know of any case of adoption. The Red-leg chick is fairly easy to distinguish as the colouring is pepper and salt rather than buff and salt. The long black bands which appear on the Grey partridge's back are reversed in value and are cream-white in the Red-leg. The first moult to full adult plumage is not quite the same as with the common partridge. Red-legs with imperfect moult being about two or three weeks later to come to really perfect plumage.

It is interesting that these birds so closely related, according to the work of systematologists, are yet so wide apart when it comes to the question of crossing. Morris and also Yale mention a cross between partridge and Red-legged partridge, but apart from the imperfectly plumaged specimens, I have never seen one, and Emilius Hopkinson's *Records of Birds Bred in Captivity* is discreetly reticent concerning partridge of any kind. There is further no reason to believe that crosses are likely between any of the indigenous forms of American game and any imported partridge stock. Even the Quail has failed to hybridise except with Quail sub-species, and this doubtfully. On the other hand cock Quail do, according to a very knowledgeable *garde champêtre*, try to tread hen partridges (Red-legs), but entirely without result.

The sexual union of any species of partridge is not generally seen. It is done in the air and is over in a flash. It is a very good test of the credibility or otherwise of anyone who chatters about birds to draw him out gently about this sexual act of partridges. If he says he has seen a cock treading a hen you can write him off as an unreliable witness!

The following summarises the difference between the two species:

The Common Partridge [*Perdix perdix* (Linnaeus), *Perdix cinerea* (La Cham)]. Length 12·5 in. Adult male, brownish buff above with narrow imbricated black crossbars. Scapulars and median wing coverts, blotched chestnut. Scalp, brown streaked buff, but remainder of head and throat warm rust-red. The breast and flanks are pale ash-grey and the centre of the breast is occupied by a chestnut-coloured horseshoe-shaped patch. Under parts, very light grey. Iris of eye, brown with small surrounding red skin area. Legs, pale slate-grey. In spring the winter plumage is much faded, and the brown seems to have washed out, by June both male and female assume an eclipse plumage and the new plumage is not complete till September or in the case of young birds October. These can, however, be distinguished from old birds by the first primary of the wing having a pointed or lancet point as distinct from round or spoon-ended feather of an old bird.

Variations in plumage in the common partridge are fairly wide. A dark red form at one time classified as *Perdix montana* is not uncommon on upland grouse country. It is a predominantly more chestnut-brown than grey bird and probably moor food conditions account for its approximation to the grouse and black game colour scheme. A pale variety albinistic in which the dark chestnut breast horseshoe is replaced by a light buff or grey buff horseshoe is not uncommon. It is not a mountain bird, seldom ranging far from valleys in Scotland, and its general limit is the border of cultivation. In Wales and England it is found up to about 1,200 feet. Its geographical distribution is approximately up to 62 degrees N. and S. to the Pyrenees and northern coasts of the Mediterranean. W., it is common in Ireland (sometimes in the dark form) and E. it extends as far as the Altai mountains. In Spain, North Africa, and the Middle East it is replaced by the Red-legged species.

The egg colour varies from the usual olive-brown to a light grey with a bluish tint. The average size is 1·38 × 1·05. The average clutch is fourteen to fifteen, though heavier nests are not rare in a favourable season. Laying begins in England in a normal spring about the second to third week of April, later by two weeks or so in Scotland. The incubation period is variable; dated eggs may, in my experience, run as short as twenty-two days or as long as twenty-five. This is, I think, in some way due to the weather and temperature prevailing during the period of exposure of the eggs. This takes place when the hen decides she has a full clutch and decides to sit. Until then the eggs are kept covered, but for a day they are left exposed.

In practice one can allow forty-four days for the completion of the whole process of laying and incubation. The eggs are laid (if not interrupted by cold spells) at the rate of one to every one-and-a-half days, and fifteen eggs will be laid in twenty days, with a further twenty-four for incubation. Early broods may appear by the first week of June, but the bulk of the hatch occurs about June 21 to 25.

The Red-legged or French partridge [*Caccabis rufa* (Linnaeus) or *Alectoris rufa*]. Length 13·5 in. Both sexes alike in plumage. Males distinguished by flat ergot or spur plate on leg. No seasonal variation of feathering. The scalp is grey with a white eyebrow. The beak and skin patches round the eye are bright red as are the legs. The throat is white joining a marked collar of black-tipped feathers over a red-brown shoulder and a pale lavender-grey breast. The flanks are of the same lavender grey, but richly barred with white, chestnut, and black. The back is red-brown and the belly a light buff. Juvenile birds are a plain indifferentiated grey-brown with no red or black bars or striations. The feathers are white-spotted at the top and tail feathers brown with black mottles. The head of the chick is chestnut with black points.

The egg is 1·6 × 1·2, variable in colour from dark brown to yellow buff and mottled with fine red-brown spots or occasionally larger blotches. It is larger and harder shelled than that of the common partridge. The incubation period is a day less than that of the ordinary partridge in any given season. Laying begins slightly earlier, but owing to the tendency to lay two nests, one of which may be deserted—or may be hatched by the cock— the main hatch is about mid-June. It is quite true that we do not know a great deal about the habits of the Red-legged partridge. Some birds will desert at the slightest interference, others will nest in a garden and almost seek human society. It is unsafe to generalise from individual experience about this bird.

It is not essentially a bird dependent on cultivation, but is probably at its best just beyond the fringe of cultivation and in hill country. Although technically a "partridge," it is probably closer to the francolin species than *Perdix*. No cross with common partridge is known. The common Grey partridge is almost voiceless, but the Red-leg makes a distinct "chuck-chuck" like its brother the Chukor. The northern limit is roughly Holland, but S. and E. related birds are world-wide in distribution.

In Great Britain a century or more ago we had a certain amount of Quail. To-day they are, to all intents and purposes, extinct as a breeding species. There may be, now and then,

a nest in Hampshire or East Anglia, and I have heard Quail "call" in England. The balance of probability is that they are not quite extinct and that an occasional westward swing of migration brings us a few, breeding birds. These leave us before partridge shooting (which begins legally on September 1st, but is not in serious swing till some weeks later) is really operative. An English gun surprising a bevy of Quail would not, unless he had shot Quail abroad, recognise them and would consider them a late brood of partridge too small to be shot! At least that is what I hope would be the natural reaction of a sportsman. If he recognised them as Quail also he would not shoot, in the hope that they might return and breed again next year. Vain hope, perhaps, but there is more to be said for the code of sportsmen than for that of politicians.

The Common Quail [*Coturnix coturnix* (Linnaeus)] is simply a miniature partridge, as is also the American Bob White Quail. I am told on very serious, though unveracious authority, that the call of the Quail indigenous to the Southern States of the Union is more melodious, but as the same authority identified a corncrake as "a school marm from Kansas," I suspect some local prejudice rather than a very precise ear.

Quail, when they come, are far later in laying and hatching than either of our partridges. By then the corn is high and we see next to nothing of them. You may hear them, but the ordinary Englishman who has not heard them abroad would not notice it. They range on occasion right up to the north of Scotland and are reported from the Orkneys. Once they were common in Ireland, but there is no country where realities become legends more swiftly. I do not know and, so far as I know, nobody knows if we could get Quail to become again summer migrants breeding in the British Isles.

In the past we blamed the reduction of Quail on the wholesale Italian slaughter of these birds on migration. Mussolini is supposed to have put a stop to that. Great Britain has not, however, placed its entire faith in the conduct of contemporary princes and has passed an Act prohibiting the import of live Quails. Chilled or frozen Quail is not worth eating, and our very sensible bird policy is to restrict in every way any commercial exploitation of birds as an article of food interesting and profit-making to men of business. If it becomes unprofitable to net Quails—well the bottom drops out of the business and the English point of view is *not* to restrict legitimate sport, but to stop the exploitation of migrant birds, whether Quails or duck, by commercial interests.

There is, I believe, an old French proverb that "the best sauce for a hare is to have shot it oneself!" It would perhaps be best for the ducks and game-birds which are migratory (not the pheasant which we can rear, or any bird whose supply we can control) if a general international law were agreed stopping all sale! You may shoot your own game—you may give away surplus—but no commercial enterprise should be allowed to market game. If we took the profit out of it, Nature would probably redress the balance within a period of years.

There are species of Quail, almost a dozen of them, and three or four have been successfully bred in aviaries. Very little is on record about hybrids, but the Californian crested quail is noted as having raised fertile hybrids with the scaly-breasted Colin. Both are American game-birds. The Chinese painted quail breeds well, but does not cross so far as is known, but in a country where common Quail are successful, straight introductions are always worth exploring.   The work of Mr. Herbert L. Stoddard of the Bureau of Biological Survey (Scribner 1931) is the fullest possible work on the Bob-white and the Mexican Quail.   It is an admirable book in that it is a very fine practical piece of work covering an enormous ecological field.   It is perhaps less scientifically specialised than similar European investigations—but pure science is not as a rule very useful in providing practical help. On the other hand, the conquest of human disease is proceeding so rapidly that we need all the ground work possible in avian disease, and if we could see far enough into the future, the microscope is probably going to be the greatest weapon for the preservation of bird life and game conservation.

Well over ninety per cent of game-chicks die of parasitic disease coccidiosis—a protozoan —or strongyle or larger worms.   A specific chemical able to destroy the eggs or oocysts of these parasites would be an incomparable boon to poultry farmers and game raisers.   It is always a possibility, hopefully a probability, that a bio-chemist may find a new synthetic compound which will literally get under the skin of these parasites and kill them.   Experimental work with some of the dyes which are used by microscopists to stain them are promising. Nothing obviously can control wild conditions, but it may within a few years be possible to dress "feed" in game farms so as to produce something like immunity from parasitic disease. From such "Heating Centres" it may be possible to reintroduce economically a large proportion of the bird life the last two human generations let slip.

In England we have lost or nearly lost Quail—but it may be possible to reintroduce and foster an indigenous species—if we could control parasitic disease.   The Quail has not, I think, been extinguished in England by the overseas toll.   That is a bad thing, but I am permitted to put forward a hypothesis.   It is that the Quail is subject to all partridge diseases.   It hatches later than the partridge when there are more flies and insects about. The increase in our partridge population has been enormous since 1830 and the ratio of possible parasitic infection astonishingly increased.   I can find no real reason for the extinction of Quail in Great Britain other than avian disease.   And I think that people who consider the introduction of any species of partridge, Grey or Red-leg, had better carry this idea of mine very much in mind—lest they should by introducing Partridge reduce indigenous Quail.

PHEASANTS: A DIAGRAM OF VARIETIES

Top left, MONGOLIAN (*P. Mongolicus*). *Top right*, JAPANESE
(*P. Versicolor*). *Centre*, MELANISTIC MUTANT (*P. Tenebrosus*).
Below left, OLD ENGLISH (*P. Colchicus*). *Below, right*, CHINESE
(*P. Torquatus*).

PHEASANT

THE most important game-bird is the pheasant. It has the sovereign virtue of enormous adaptability to surroundings and will in a very short time be the best distributed sporting bird in the world. The original European pheasant is *Phasianus colchicus*, and is a bird with a black neck free from the white ring which distinguishes other sub-species. Traditionally its origin is from the River Phasis and the valleys of the district of Colchis, near to the Black Sea. Actually, though, the bird occurs in a wild state westward to the Dalmatian shore and it is advisable to remember that it is essentially a bird which does well in rather damp surroundings and is far less dependent on a dry brood rearing season than, for instance, the partridge.

Tradition ascribes the introduction of the pheasant to the British Isles to the Romans, but this is probably quite incorrect. The bird is not shown in any of the early Celtic illuminated manuscript, and as the fullest possible use is made of animal motifs in these works it is hardly possible that the pheasant could have been overlooked as it is a bird of immediate appeal to an artist.

The earliest reference to the pheasant in England which has come down to us is the record of ration allowances to certain ecclesiastical canons about to celebrate the feast of St. Michael in 1059. It is worth quoting from Harting and Tegetmuir: "Erant autem tales pitantiae unicuique canonico; a festo Sancti Michaelis usque ad caput jejunii, aut XII merulae aut ii *agansea* aut ii perdices *aut unus phasianus*, reliquis temporibus aut ancae aut gallinae."

In English, the good men were entitled to a ration of twelve larks or two *agansea*. This word has bothered translators for half a century, and the nearest they could get to it was "magpies," whose quick, agitated movement of the tail gives us the French word *agacer* the jitters. Recently I found out that a Spanish word for moor-hens was *agazer* and it seems pretty clear now that moor-hens was the edible meant as an alternative to the two partridges or one pheasant. This is, I think, my only useful contribution to philology.

At any rate, pheasant was on the English menu before Harold fell at Senlac, and the rate of progress from the relatively civilised epicentre in the south of England is not easy to assess. All we can say is that it was established in Ireland by about 1500, but did not become common in Scotland much before 1594. In those days it took the bird some five hundred years to reach and pass the Border. This seems an incredibly slow rate of progress, but we must remember that Britain then bristled with every kind of vermin, there was no close season, and a bird was simply so much potential food. There were no arms of precision, and though a bow and arrow is quite effective for hitting deer, birds were small targets and scarce warranted the cost of a shaft. Most bird catching was done with nets or traps, and it is not until about the first third of the eighteenth century that the art of wing shooting became practical.

By this time the second species of pheasant, the Chinese pheasant (*P. torquatus*) with a white neck ring was introduced about 1700. There is no exact date for it, but it came in with tea, japanned or lacquer furniture in the Chinese taste, and porcelain. These birds brought back by the sea captains were just aviary birds, but they soon began interbreeding with the old English blacknecks, and hybrids appeared. It is difficult to determine when the ringneck established ascendancy over the blackneck, but so far as I can judge from old pictures and sporting prints, this predominancy did not occur till about one hundred and fifty years after the introduction.

By the mid-Victorian period, when the breech-loader was just beginning to supplant the muzzle-loader, the hybrid ringneck begins to appear in prints and pictures as a typical pheasant. Its extension to the north seems to have been checked and even to-day there are parts of Scotland where the indigenous wild pheasant is predominantly the old black-neck or Colchicus type. In 1840 a third sub-species was introduced: the Japanese or Versicolor pheasant. The original pair was a gift from the King of Italy to the Earl of Derby. They flourished and multiplied and presumably there were other importations, but by about 1860 the crossbred Versicolor was the commonest type of pheasant in East Anglia, though not widely distributed in the south and west.

It did not prove a very useful bird. It is small and nervous and it was fairly rapidly submerged in the common blackneck × ringneck. It flourished for a time and then left no visible trace except for a point which will be discussed later under the melanistic mutant.

About 1900 the late Carl Hagenbeck, the great animal and menagerie dealer, introduced a new sub-species, the Mongolian pheasant (*P. c. mongolicus*). It was a very light coloured and large bird of the Chinese kind, but with a broken or interrupted neck ring. It is a little difficult to determine what effect this bird had on the previous introductions. My own opinion—and it is purely opinion—is that the Mongolian was the most valuable of all introductions because before this we had a tradition that pheasants were very delicate birds and needed a very expensive and difficult upbringing.

These ideas dominated for the first decade of the twentieth century. Pheasants were fed on extraordinary diets of custard and eggs, and no one can look back upon what passed for wisdom and sound sense in the year nineteen hundred without a scientific shudder.

The diets advocated were wholly out of balance, and it is no wonder that the mortality index of delicateness in pheasants was a peak exceeding Mount Everest. We hatched pheasants in large numbers and killed them off with the stupidest and most expensive foods. The elements of animal nutrition were not understood and when the European War occurred and the keepers had to leave their usual employment to shoot Germans, the pheasant, left to itself, proved not to be a delicate bird, but a really tough sort of bird able to get along better without the witch-dancing ignorance of the keepers' trade.

The birds survived no-keepering, increased and flourished, and from the time of the War one can date a very much newer and clearer application of the nutritional needs of the birds. We still know remarkably little about the real science, for arguments derived from domestic poultry are not applicable to the pheasant. It is a bird which needs not only a higher meat or insect-food intake than the fowl, but it needs and must have a higher intake of green food which is a source of Vitamin B. I have experimented with pheasants raised on wire which could never come into contact with real earth and could not be contaminated from their own droppings, but eventually those pheasants have got to be put on earth and relegated to the coverts.

From a purely scientific point of view it is possible to bring up pheasants on a carefully balanced diet with practically no losses—but when you turn them out they are more susceptible to disease. The balance of probability suggests that the pheasant is better equipped to resist disease if it is not wholly artificially fed on a diet composed of the best scientific material. It would seem, in practice, that contact with mother earth was necessary and that young pheasants are better off with a mild injection of the ailments they are likely to encounter later in life.

Many develop a natural resistance and are "allergic" to most common troubles in the way of parasitic disease if the purely scientific control is relaxed and they are allowed to have fresh-cut turves to pick at.

A turf is obviously the harbourer of all sorts of infections; it contains so many unknowns that it knocks the logical bottom out of any feeding experiment, but if we can draw the inference that a limited infection is good practice it is difficult to explain the effect. My opinion (which I may have to qualify in years to come) is based on work in progress. I think that pheasants for sport can be reared on wire with a good diet, but that all that is known about nutrition does not quite meet the situation. The nigger in the wood-pile is that the purely artificially fed and raised bird is not sufficiently resistant to infection when it leaves its experimental environment and comes into contact with the wild.

The probable solution is to allow the birds to get a mild infection and develop their own immunity, but this introduces an uncontrollable and scientifically immeasurable element. As things now stand pheasants are reared in much the same way as they were a hundred and fifty years ago, and it is very doubtful indeed if most modern proprietary food preparations are half as good as the older natural grain and greenstuff diets. We now know the importance of "whole" grain (that is corn not deprived of its bran or germ) and the very serious need of the pheasant for about twice as much Vitamin B group of accessory food factors as is required by ordinary poultry.

The pheasant is a bird of surprises, but the greatest surprise was the breeding of a new sub-species from birds in England. It is a dark-plumaged bird and is labelled *Phasianus mut. tenebrosus*; it is the melanistic mutant just as an albino pheasant is an albinistic mutant, but the odd thing about it is that it is a true sub-species in that it breeds true for generations. It is claimed by some zoologists that it is a really true sub-species, but the whole affair is obscure and a good many practical naturalists and game farmers hold that it is the outcrop of latent Japanese or *P. versicolor* blood in the common mongrel ordinary pheasant. The late Lord Rothschild held that there was only *one* species of pheasant (*P. colchicus*), and that all the sub-species were simply local forms or variations. Mr. William Beebe, author of the *Monograph of the Pheasants*, holds that there are two types—the Asiatic pheasant or blackneck (*P. colchicus*) and the Japanese pheasant (*P. versicolor*).

3

The latter represents an island form separated for long from the parent stock and certainly seems to be a distinct bird where the variations of known pheasants given rank as sub-species on plumage characteristics may be thirty-five or so before one reaches the opposite pole occupied by the blackneck. The plumage of the Common Versicolor is so close to that of the mutant that many birds of the latter variety were sold by game farmers as cross Versicolors. An interesting point is that this dark form or mutant is believed to have occurred before in the early 'eighties, specimens were known to Lord Rothschild. It is a very curious thing that about thirty to forty years after a small "boom" in Versicolors which stock is in the process of time absorbed into the "ordinary" or mongrel pheasant this dark mutation occurs. The balance of probability points to the first crop of mutants being shot and only remarked on as oddities. Chance allowed straight aviary line breeding of the second appearance of the variety. The history of the breed is so far as is known that eggs were sold by the original Liphook Game Farm to a General Roudell, in Yorkshire, who later exchanged some eggs with C. G. Talbot Ponsonby. Those eggs hatched these odd dark birds and Talbot Ponsonby bred them for fifteen years and presented birds to the Zoological Society of London where they have been successfully bred for years and found, under aviary conditions, to breed true.

A very large number of pure mutant and ×-mutant eggs have been sold by game farms, but so far as one can see they are again disappearing and becoming submerged in the "ordinaries." Theoretically they ought to breed true, but although they obey Mendel's laws quite nicely in aviaries the introduction of this strain of dark blood does not show up very much among pheasants under natural conditions.

I can advance no explanation other than a theory that the melanistic mutant like the albino is not a very dominant sexual success. Pheasant hens are open to the attentions of any male bird and the males are more than polygamous, they are really worthy of the name Asiatic pheasant! For some reason or other the dark bird does not seem to be able to compete with his tough Aryanised brother, and where I introduced mutants some five years ago they were rare last season.

There are various ways of determining the difference of plumage between a mutant and a versicolor, but when you come to the crosses it needs a good cabinet zoologist to decide. For general sporting purposes the soles of the feet are the quickest index. With the dark mutant these are pink on the palmar surfaces, chocolate brown elsewhere. In fact just like the human negro!

It is quite possible that the widespread introduction of the pheasant into the United States may produce new sub-species. There have been two historic pioneer introductions. Benjamin Franklin's son, who was a Loyalist, imported pheasants from England to the eastern coast. Later, pheasants were imported in the west and spread throughout Oregon. In the United States, pheasants are believed to be Chinese, but it is quite clear that the original Franklin introduction must have been the English mixed breed which was at that time only slightly mixed with ringneck blood. To-day State game farms and private farms get most of their eggs from Europe and in a decade or so the obliging pheasant has begun to replace the indigenous game which had been dispossessed as much by the advance of "development" as by the uncontrolled activities of the "man with the gun."

PHEASANTS: CHILBOLTON DOWN

Conditions in the United States will not parallel those in Great Britain for many years. The pheasant has to fight an uphill battle in a country of far wider climatic variations, against a balance of vermin unbelievable to an English or Scotch gamekeeper and with a wholly different type of insects and vegetable foods. Yet such is the adaptability of the bird that he acclimatises perfectly, and in a very few generations of pheasants there will be no doubt about his adjustment to conditions throughout woodland and upland in the temperate zones.

There is already, thanks to State game conservation effort, a coast to coast distribution, and eventually only prairie and desert belts will be without some wild pheasants. These areas are in any case more suited to other types of bird such as the partridge and related Chukor who can stand aridity, the pheasant is, however, primarily a bird of swamps, river-bottom lands, or damp mountain forest. In ten years to come the pheasant distribution map of the U.S.A. and Canada will be astonishingly interesting.

There are other pheasant sub-species, and there are a number of birds which are not true pheasants but which are classed with them, such as the *Chrysolophus amherstiae*, or Amherst pheasant, and allied species. Many of these are not more than rare "collectors' birds" from almost unexplored mountain country between five and nine thousand feet high, but it is more than probable that acclimatised in a suitable environment and at a suitable elevation, rarities which have proved of little use as game, or have been purely bred as ornamental fowl, might do well.

The true pheasants cross easily and their hybrids are as a rule fertile, but though first crosses of true pheasants and allied species are fairly commonly recorded, these hybrids do not as a rule possess fertility and are mules. In the same way crosses between similar allied species such as *Chrysolophus amherstiae* and *Chrysolophus pictus*, the Golden pheasant, are successful and breed true, indeed most Golden pheasants now have an Amherst strain in them, but so far I believe I am right in saying that no fertile hybrid has been derived from Amherst × Versicolor though the cross has been successfully made.

The pheasant and the partridge may seem to be very different birds to the sportsman, but the ornithologist knows that it is rather hard to say where the sub-family Phasianinae begins to change into the sub-family Perdicinae, for it is best to envision them all as one class under the heading of game-birds. When we consider various Indian birds it is not too easy to decide whether a bird is nearer in cousinship to the pheasant or to the partridge! In general, though, all the pheasants are relatively large birds with a wing over eight inches long, and in the vast majority the tail is longer than the wing. In the case of the Perdicinae this is reversed. Unfortunately no very accurate way of dividing the game-birds has been wholly agreed. Beebe suggested in 1914 a classification based on the order in which certain feathers are moulted. It did not receive universal support as it is not a very useful guide to the sportsman, and it is not free from exceptions.

Probably the best, if perhaps not the most scientific way of arranging a sort of "key to the game-birds," is that suggested by Stuart Baker in his *Game Birds of India*. He adopts two main groups and divides the family of *Phasianidae* into two groups divided by large ocelli on tail or tail covert.

Group A—

    (*a*) wing over fifteen inches: sub-family *Pavoninae*, or Peafowl group.

    (*b*) wing less than fifteen inches: sub-family *Argusaininae*, or Argus pheasant group.

Group B, with no ocellations—

    (*c*) wing over eight inches; tail longer than wing except in *Lophophorus* and *Lophura*: sub-family *Phasianinae*, Pheasant group.

    (*d*) wing under eight inches except *Tragopan*, *Ithaginis*, and *Tetraogallus*, tail much shorter than wing except in *Tragopan* (in which tail and wing are equal): sub-family *Perdicinae*, Partridge group.

This key allows one to tell fairly well where a bird should be placed, but in practice we find that a very much closer sub-division of sub-species is necessary before fertile cross-breeding can take place.

It will be wiser not to introduce the wider varieties of pheasants into this chapter, for they are still technically birds for aviaries or zoological gardens rather than general acclimatisation. The true game pheasants in Great Britain and in general introduction in the United States are as follows:

1. The ordinary or common pheasant which is predominantly a mongrel, merging *P. colchicus* and *P. torquatus* with introductions of the blood of *P. mongolicus* and *P. versicolor*, which latter two are recessive and usually lost in succeeding generations, is sometimes called *P. colchicus torquatus* (Gmelin). But the name is not in common scientific usage. Actually it is never easy to be sure of the contributory factors in the mongrel type until the pure stocks are noted for their essential differences.

Taking these in order of European introduction we begin with *P. colchicus*, called the Old English Blackneck.

P. colchicus, male. Eyes yellow-gold with a scarlet patch of bare skin finely mottled with black. In the breeding season these "wattles" fill and also carry small erectile patches of short purple feathers like "ears" or "horns." The upper part of the head and neck is apparently black, but actually a deep purple with an occasional green gleam according to the incidence of the angle of light. The breast is the familiar golden colour, but many of the feathers are dark purple tipped. The rump is dark chestnut and the small feathers of the wing a light brown or buff. The tail feathers are deep greeny-brown, cross-barred with narrow black bands and edged with red-brown.

The female. Upper part predominantly *café-au-lait* fawn mottled with dark brown and black; lower part and abdomen very light fawn.

P. torquatus, male. Differs from the above by a white collar or ring encircling the whole neck, white eyebrows and a grey to lavender rump. The shorter wing feathers are also lavender grey and the black crossbars on the tail are broader. All pheasants hailing from east of a line from the Altai to Chittagong have this blue to olive or lavender grey rump, while birds from west of this line are predominantly buff or rufous rumped.

The female. Difficult to distinguish from hen of *colchicus*.

P. mongolicus, male. A rather deeper and less copper-red general body colour with a light yellow rather than golden iris to the eye. No ear tufts of feather on the wattles. The white neck ring is broken in front and the small feathers of the wings are often nearly white. The impression given by pure Mongolians and first cross Mongolians is of a larger but lighter-plumaged type of bird.

The female. Much lighter coloured than hen *colchicus*. Eyes, lemon yellow.

P. versicolor, male. A distinctive bottle-green bird with dark purple head and neck, no neck ring. Wing feathers greenish to lavender, but marked with chestnut and fawn. Rump lavender to green, tail greenish to light grey, barred purplish black.

The female. A small dark bird with the darker feathers of the mottling almost chocolate.

P. tenebrosus (mut.) male. It is not easy to distinguish at first from the Versicolor cock, has a brown olive rather than a lavender bluish rump, pale brown wing coverts, and dark legs with pink soles. White traces appear on the neck, but a full or partial ring is unusual. Light yellow flecks may appear on flank feathers, but the general appearance of the whole bird is darker and less green than the Versicolor. The lower body plumage is often a dark, smoky grouse colour.

The female. Resembles closely a grouse in general colouring. The feathers are deep chocolate, barred black and edged faint buff. Chicks have chocolate down.

WILD TURKEY

RUFFED GROUSE

WILD TURKEY

GREAT BRITAIN has never possessed such a grand game-bird as the Wild Turkey though perhaps the Great Bustard, now lost to this country for over a hundred years, may lay claim to something approaching the same noble dignity and magnificent demeanour. The Wild Turkey belongs to the same sub-family as the Pheasants, of which the Guinea-fowls are also members and its nearest relations. The bird which has been domesticated in Europe and is now so generally connected with the Christmas feast, is the typical Mexican "Pavo" or "Guajhalote," *Meleagris g. gallopavo*, with white tips to the tail feathers and tail coverts. The race occurring in North America, *Meleagris g. americana*, is distinguished by the chestnut-brown tips to tail and tail coverts. The Wild Turkey is a forest bird and likes the parts where the trees grow densest, but it will also haunt the borders of swamp land. Though at one time Wild Turkeys were abundant, they have greatly decreased in number and probably not least among the causes of this is excessive shooting.

They feed on a variety of nuts—acorns, chestnuts, and so on—seeds of many kinds, grapes, berries, and insects, being particularly addicted to grasshoppers. Though they are usually faithful to one locality, if food becomes short they will migrate on foot to another district in large flocks, but they generally return again later to their old haunts. Wild Turkey chicks do not show so much evidence of delicacy as the domesticated birds, for they are bred and reared with great success at Whipsnade Zoological Park, where they are left to the care of the hen. A wetting, however, as those who have reared domestic Turkey chicks know only too well, is almost certain to bring about fatal results, and this cause is probably also responsible for a high mortality in the wild.

According to some American writers the parental instincts of the gobbler are deplorable, for they say he will eat the eggs if he can get hold of them, and may even go so far in wrath that he is even not averse to devouring his own progeny. This cannibalistic tendency has not, however, been observed at Whipsnade, where the birds are only in semi-captivity.

The specific disease of turkey is "Blackhead," an amoeba infection of the liver, which can, however, be cured by formic acid in the meal, a fact which turkey raisers unconsciously used when they gave them chopped nettles.

WOODCOCK AND SNIPE

THE Woodcock *Scolopax rusticola* belongs to the Charadriidae, which includes the snipe and waders, but it is more essentially a woodland bird than any of the other members of this family. It has increased in numbers in Great Britain during recent years, no doubt a good deal owing to the protection afforded it during the spring. It is a somewhat solitary bird and spends the day-time hidden in a wood or sheltered hill-side, flying to some marshy place to feed at dusk. Its extremely effective protective coloration renders it almost invisible among dead leaves and undergrowth. The nest, which is usually in some sheltered situation in a wood, is a mere depression in the ground, lined with dead leaves. Usually one, but frequently two, broods are produced during the season.

The Woodcock is a somewhat silent bird except during the spring when the cocks are "roding"—flying slowly to and fro in open spaces and rides among the trees, at about thirty feet from the ground, uttering a deep, and also a sharp, chirping note. There appears to be a good deal of movement among Woodcock and a great fluctuation in numbers. Some of the British birds are resident, others are summer visitors arriving in early spring and leaving again in August; but by far the largest number are winter visitors which arrive from the Continent from September onwards, and leave again for their summer quarters in northern Europe from the end of March and May. They migrate in large flocks and sometimes the immigrations are quite impressive. The Woodcock and its migrations are a subject which present a great deal of scope for further study, and the British Trust for Ornithology instituted a special inquiry into its general habits and movements which has resulted in a good deal of further information concerning this interesting and somewhat secretive bird.

The renowned habit of the Woodcock of carrying its young is still disputed by some naturalists, but it has been actually witnessed by so many reliable observers that there seems little doubt about it. The fact that this performance is usually carried out in the very early hours of the morning or at dusk may account for so few people having seen it. Personally, I believe that there is far more carrying of young by parent birds than is generally credited. The chick is carried between the legs and thighs of the parent Woodcock, pressed close up to the body, and in some way the old bird bends its toes round to prevent the youngster from falling.

The food consists mostly of earthworms which the bird procures by probing the mud with its specially adapted, sensitive beak, insects of various kinds, and small mollusca.

The American Woodcock *Philohela minor* is smaller than the European bird and has not any of the cross-barring on the underparts; this is replaced by a uniform colour of soft reddish-yellow. Its habitat is similar to that of the European Woodwock, which it also resembles in general behaviour. American naturalists also credit their bird with the habit of carrying its young. It is comparatively scarce and is confined to Eastern North America, north to southern Canada. The great reduction in numbers is attributed to indiscriminate shooting, for cultivation of land can have had little influence upon its breeding grounds. Woodcock may still be legally shot under the terms of the Migratory Birds Convention Act.

Great Britain's only breeding Snipe, the Common Snipe, *Capella gallinago*, is fairly plentiful all over the British Isles in the marshy or moist localities that suit it, though it is scarcer in some southern counties. The numbers are greatly increased in autumn by visitors from the Continent, some of which spend the winter and others pass through on their way south. The well-known "drumming" during the breeding season, which is produced on the downward flight in the wonderful aerial evolutions indulged in at this time, is made by the two outer feathers of the spread tail. This sound is usually likened to the bleating of a goat, but I think it is far more like the loud humming of some insect. During the spring and early summer the birds are constantly engaged in "drumming" with very little respite. I have heard and seen a Snipe engaged in this evidence of *joie-de-vivre* at 2 a.m. on a very cold June morning.

The Great Snipe, *Capella media*, is a rare passage migrant and may be seen in small parties in autumn. It is a larger and darker bird than the Common Snipe and has a great deal of white in the tail, also the underparts are more heavily barred.

The Jack Snipe, *Lymnocryptes minimus*, which is a winter visitor, is much smaller than the Common Snipe and can readily be distinguished from it. It lacks the broad pale stripe down the middle of the crown, the bill is comparatively shorter and the upper plumage has a greenish-purple sheen. It also has not the characteristic zigzag flight of the Common Snipe, and is reluctant to rise. There have been various reports of Jack Snipe nesting in Great Britain, but these have not been authenticated. A few birds may stay through the summer—I have flushed one as late as the second half of May.

The American Wilson's Snipe, *Capella delicata*, as its name indicates, is of very fine flavour and a favourite sporting bird. It is similar both in appearance and habits to the Common Snipe of the Old World, and is commonly, though incorrectly, called "Jack Snipe."

Though Woodcock and Snipe are popular game-birds in Great Britain the law does not recognise them as such. There are two sets of laws dealing with birds in the British Isles, the Game Acts which originated in the reign of Henry VII, and the Wild Birds Protection Acts, the first of which was passed in 1880. Both Woodcock and Snipe are considered as "Wild Birds," and therefore do not enjoy the special privileges accorded to game-birds. The Woodcock, at any rate, seems to have done very well with the protection that has been afforded it under the Wild Birds Protection Acts, but the arrangement is confusing.

The preservation of both game and wild birds is a question that is now being dealt with on more practical and scientific lines by most countries of the world. Conditions have changed so rapidly within the last century that measures which were quite adequate fifty

Woodcock

years ago are now quite out of date in view of modern requirements. As so many birds are migratory their preservation is being regarded more and more from the international point of view, and this is heading to a goal most satisfactory to all; for it is manifestly unfair that one country should destroy without restraint what another nation has bred and produced. However, in the preservation of birds, as in all things, varying conditions must play a large part. It is a general impulse to blame and condemn "the foreigner," but national temperaments and customs should also be taken into consideration. Many Englishmen look with horror on the custom, which is carried on in some European countries, of shooting cock Capercaillie when they are displaying. On the other hand, a Bulgarian once said to me, "I can hardly believe the British to be so unsporting, they actually shoot Capercaillie *on the wing*!" To his mind any other method than stalking a sitting bird was despicable. Though the fundamental rule of giving all birds peace during the *entire* breeding season is the most sensible and practical one from the majority of points of view, if the system of stalking and shooting Capercaillie in Central Europe were prohibited, the bird might possibly eventually die out altogether in those countries, for few people would then be sufficiently interested to keep up its numbers by careful preservation and encouragement during the rest of the year.

EUROPEAN
WIGEON   SCAUP

AMERICAN
PINTAIL

GREEN-WINGED TEAL   LESSER SCAUP

GEESE AND DUCKS

WILD geese and ducks have a wide and diverse appeal—to sportsmen, to naturalists, to aviculturists and to those who simply wish to look at something beautiful, wildfowl fulfil a need. Wild goose and wild duck shooting have a fascination entirely their own; the loneliness, the difficulties and the pure beauty of the surroundings, combined are something difficult to equal. To the naturalist the study of the appearance, the habits, the complicated and decorative courtship displays and the amazing migrations are a source of never-ending interest. There is nothing more satisfying in aviculture than keeping wildfowl on a pond, and their beauty of form and colouring are a delight even to those who can barely distinguish a duck from a goose.

An enormous amount of literature has been written, and continues to be written, on wildfowl, for its appeal is ever growing. It is impossible in a short space to give more than a fleeting impression of the interest of this fascinating group of birds.

Wild geese and ducks belong to the family of the Anatidae which also includes swans. The geese and duck members of this family are divided into a number of sub-families of which among geese the *Anserinae*, or true geese, are perhaps the best known. Geese have a world-wide distribution, in most cases breeding in the far north and coming to warmer latitudes in winter. Several species are common both to America and England though differing slightly in form. Great Britain has only one breeding goose, the Grey Lag, *Anser anser*, and in America also all but one nest in arctic regions. This species, the Canada Goose, *Branta canadensis*, is confined to North America and is the most well known of all geese there. It has been divided into five sub-species—the Honker, *Branta c. canadensis*, Lesser Canada Goose, *B. c. leucopareia*, Western Goose, *B. c. occidentalis*, Hutchin's Goose, *B. c. hutchinsi*, and the Cackling Goose, *B. c. minima*. The Canada Goose, which does very well in captivity, has been introduced into Great Britain though without great success; it is, however, semi-domesticated in one or two localities.

Geese are more land-lubbers than duck and whereas the sexes in most species of duck show great differences in plumage, in geese they are alike. There is also very little seasonal change in goose plumage. Geese migrate in pairs or families and are capable of travelling great distances uninterruptedly. John Phillips calculated that Canada Geese may travel a thousand miles without a stop.

As geese are universal so are wild ducks, which are found throughout the world wherever there is suitable feeding and nesting grounds for them. They breed throughout the northern hemisphere and range from the arctic north to Africa and India. In the New World they winter from the northern States to the great Central Valley in Mexico, and many species are represented in southern South America.

Ducks are usually active in the early morning and evening, and spend the greater part of the day resting; a good many will feed at night, particularly if there is moonlight. They are extremely wary, but this is no doubt owing a great deal to persecution, for young ducks are confiding little creatures and adult birds soon respond to a feeling of security. Dr. Leonard Gill, Director of the South African Museum at Cape Town, has drawn attention to the great tameness of wildfowl when they arrive in South Africa on the lakes where they are not molested, and the Mallard in England has become in some instances such a complete Londoner as to convey her family across main streets, waiting for the policeman on point duty to hold up the traffic.

Most ducks nest on the ground, some build nests actually on the water, whereas others choose trees. In most of the northern ducks the male abandons the female as soon as the young are hatched, or even as soon as incubation commences. Some species, however, have a strong sense of duty and protect the duck while she is sitting and assist with the youngsters; this is frequently the case in species where the male and female have similar plumage.

The migration of ducks is one of the most interesting problems of bird behaviour, for it appears to vary greatly. Much has been found out by ringing these birds, but an enormous amount remains to be discovered. The majority of species are migratory, though a certain percentage of individuals of some species appear to be sedentary. It is probable that the drakes follow the ducks, so that a drake hatched in one country may, in the next year, migrate to an entirely different locality with the duck of his choice.

There is considerable controversy as to whether ducks have a keen sense of smell; many ornithologists doubt this. But decoy-men carry a lump of burning peat as part of their equipment, and as the art of decoying has been handed down through generations of men who spend their whole lives in the haunts of wildfowl, it would appear they do not do this to no purpose.

The methods of shooting and hunting duck are manifold, with boats, dogs, decoys, baits, and punts. Ducks have undoubtedly been caught since the dim ages, and probably in the bad old days they were taken in the moult as being then easiest to catch. Ducks were able to stand up to shooting and catching so long as they had sufficient breeding and feeding grounds, but with the rapid progress of civilisation, conditions are not what they were and the number of adverse factors weighing against wildfowl has tipped the scale against them with a serious drop. Both in the Old World and the New widespread anxiety is being felt for the future stock of wildfowl. Primitive man may have completely disregarded the advisability of a close time, but he did not develop the arctic areas, drain marshes, rush about to wildfowl haunts in a motor-car, have breech-loaders, and all the other modern facilities, nor, most important of all, was he so numerous. Not so long ago decoys, at which thousands upon thousands of duck were caught annually, flourished in various parts of Europe. The decline in the number of decoys is but another indication of the diminishing numbers of wildfowl. At one time there were two hundred decoys in Great Britain, whereas at the present day only four are in full use. In Holland, however, large numbers of decoys continue to operate.

Top two:
SHOVELER

Next two:
BLACK DUCK

Next four:
MALLARD

GADWALL

Ducks have been divided into several different sub-families, and John Phillips divides them as follows: *Dendrocygninae*—tree ducks; *Anatinae*—surface-feeding, river or pond ducks; *Fuligulinae*—diving ducks; *Erismaturinae*—spiny-tailed ducks, which are characterised by their stiff tails; *Merganettinae*, which are grebe-like divers; and *Merginae*, which are fish-eating, have slender bodies, and toothed bills.

It is only possible, for lack of space, to mention briefly some species of the two most popular sub-families, the surface-feeding and the diving ducks.

The most typical members of the sub-family *Anatinae* are those of the genus *Anas*. These birds obtain their food on or near the surface of the water but do not dive, though certain species "end-up" in the water. The young, on the other hand, are able to dive. Of the genus the Mallard or Green Head, *Anas platyrhnychos*, frequently called *the* Wild Duck is the most well known. It has one of the widest ranges of any species and occurs throughout the greater part of the northern hemisphere. Though a fresh-water duck, it is very adaptable and can get on in any sort of country, even on tidal estuaries. It does not, as a rule, congregate in big flocks, and in flight the large size and colour of the male, and the light colour and white wing-bars of the female are a ready means of identification. It is the main British breeding duck and in a good many localities is artificially raised, but the diminishing numbers give rise to considerable concern. Though the Mallard usually nests on the ground it will sometimes select a tree. The American bird is slightly larger. The Black Duck or Black Mallard, *Anas rubripes*, occurs only in North America. It is also found in a great variety of country, but prefers to be near the sea. In many respects it is very similar in habits to the Mallard. The female, however, does not differ from the male, though she is slightly smaller. In flight Black Duck can be distinguished from Mallard as they are much darker than either male or female Mallard.

The Gadwall, Gray Duck or Speckle Belly, *Anas strepera*, has a breeding range all over the Northern hemisphere in temperate regions, but is almost everywhere an uncommon bird. It is a resident and winter visitor to the British Isles where it has bred regularly since it was artificially introduced to breed in 1850. It is essentially a fresh-water bird and prefers sheltered situations with plenty of cover. It feeds mostly on leaves and stems of aquatic plants. The female is very like the male in plumage, but her call is like that of the duck Mallard, whereas the male Gadwall has a hoarse croak. In flight the Gadwall can be most readily identified by the white ends of the secondaries, which look like a gap in the wings as it flies away.

The Wigeon, *Anas penelope*, occurs in Europe and Asia. In Britain it is a winter visitor and passage migrant though a certain number nest in Scotland. It prefers broad waters and likes open seas. It is very dependent on feeding conditions, and where these are good enormous flocks will congregate. In flight it continually utters a whistling note. On the breeding areas, which are mainly in the far north, it affects wooded or partially wooded country.

The American Wigeon or Baldpate, *Anas americana*, is confined to North America, where the breeding grounds are chiefly in western Canada. It is far more of a fresh-water bird than the European Wigeon, and is largely a vegetable feeder; it grazes more on grass than other American ducks. It does not call so frequently as the European bird and its note is more musical. The male can most readily be distinguished by his white head-band.

The Common Teal, *Anas crecca*, occurs throughout Europe and Asia and has a very wide breeding range. It also winters in Africa and wanders occasionally to America. It likes shallow feeding grounds and boggy places and is strictly a fresh-water bird, though it will go to the sea if necessity, in the form of persecution or hard weather, insists. It is a very silent bird by day and will sit motionless for hours in contemplation. The flight, which is extremely rapid, is more reminiscent of a wader, for it darts hither and thither and will also fly close to the water. It nests in most parts of Great Britain.

The American Green-winged Teal, *Anas carolinensis*, can most readily be distinguished from the Teal by the white crescent in front of the wing; it also lacks the white line above the closed wings which is present in the fully mature European bird. It is confined to North America and its usual breeding range does not extend east of the Great Lakes, though it will winter as far south as Mexico. In the greater part of the United States it is only a bird of passage. It is very similar in habits to the Common Teal.

The Pintail, *Anas acuta*, has an enormously wide distribution and is found throughout Europe, Asia, in parts of Africa and the greater part of North America. In America it has an extensive breeding range and is plentiful, but in Great Britain it only nests in small numbers in Scotland and is for the most part a scarce winter visitor. It likes large sheets of open water and is gregarious by nature. In flight it can be identified by the long neck and long, narrow, pointed wings. It is a very shy bird and very silent. The American race is slightly larger in size and the middle tail feathers are longer.

The American Blue-winged Teal, *Anas discors*, is one of the smallest of American duck and breeds in North America, wintering as far south as the West Indies and South America. It haunts small lakes and slow-flowing rivers, and sometimes salt marshes, preferring shallow ponds to large open waters. Its flight is similar to that of other Teal, but its small size and chalky blue on the wings are means of identification.

The Shoveler or Spoonbill, *Spatula clypeata*, has a tremendously wide range both in the Old and New Worlds, having an even wider distribution than the Mallard, though it is by no means common. It is easily recognised both on water and on the wing by its clumsy appearance and huge bill. The bill is edged with rows of bristles which act as a sieve for the ooze in which it finds its food. It haunts stagnant waters and marshes where there is plenty of mud which contains the minute vegetable and animal life on which it subsists. While floating on the water it keeps the head well drawn back with the beak either resting, or skimming the surface of the water.

The *Fuligulinae*, diving, sea or bay ducks, obtain their food by diving under water. They are different in their habits and have not the same delicacy of outline as the surface feeders; also their legs are placed farther back, which gives them a more waddling gait when on land. Though they can feed at night they are more dependent on a certain amount of daylight than are the surface feeders. They migrate, however, mostly at night.

The Canvas-back, *Nyroca vallisneria*, which is an American species and called in that country the "King of Ducks," has been given much attention by writers of every sort. Its delicacy of flavour is more prized than that of any other duck and its fame in this respect has spread to Europe. It is a fresh-water duck and does not usually go to salt water unless compelled. It has a very rapid flight and is very wild and wary. The Canvas-back,

BLUE-WINGED TEAL

Pochard, and Red-head are all very akin, both in colour scheme of plumage and general habits. The Common or European Pochard, *Nyroca ferina*, which occurs in the greater part of Europe and Asia is not, however, so wild by nature as the Canvas-back. It gathers in enormous flocks, is a true fresh-water duck and is fond of large open waters of moderate depth. It is an active diver and feeds mostly by day. In flight good means of identification are the short neck and absence of white wing-bars; the chestnut head and blackish breast of the male are also striking distinguishing marks.

The Red-head or American Pochard, *Nyroca americana*, is very similar in general habits to the Pochard. It is one of the best known of American ducks, though its range is not very wide. It is a fresh-water duck though at times is also found on salt water, but its habitat and food play such an important part that it is sporadic in appearance. In flight it is very like the Canvas-back but less steady; it is also lighter in colour.

The Ring-necked Duck, *Nyroca collaris*, is confined to North America where it is one of the rarest species. It is reminiscent of the Tufted Duck of Europe in general colour scheme. It keeps fairly strictly to fresh water and prefers sheltered situations to open stretches.

The Scaup or Broadbill, *Nyroca marila*, ranges throughout the greater part of the northern hemisphere and breeds mostly in the far north. It is a very sturdy bird and able to stand extremely cold weather. It haunts salt water, though sometimes is also found on fresh-water lakes. The Scaup differ from the Pochard group and have very broad, short bills. They usually form very large flocks and in flight there is a rustling sound from the wings. Unlike most species of diving duck they nest in colonies. There is very little difference between the Scaup of America and Europe.

The Lesser Scaup, *Nyroca affinis*, is a strictly American species and is much more numerous than Greater Scaup. It frequents both fresh and salt water and is well distributed. It is slightly smaller than the Greater Scaup and the reflections on the head are purplish instead of greenish, but it is not easy to distinguish the two birds.

In his monumental work on the ducks of the world, *A Natural History of the Ducks*, John Phillips stated, "Many keen duck shooters find themselves getting more and more sentimental as they grow older, and these are the men who originate all our worth-while reforms; not the type that has been brought up to look with holy horror on guns and shooting men." Few truer words have been written and it is without doubt that the true sportsman is the keenest and most effective preservationist, as was so conclusively proved in the case of John Phillips himself.

In the United States of America drastic steps have been taken to conserve the stock of wildfowl which has, from a multiplicity of reasons, reached a dangerously low ebb. This gloomy example has so aroused the Old World, that in nearly every country keen duck-shooters, even before they have found themselves growing old, are making efforts to conserve the stock of European wildfowl, before it is too late. Great Britain has recently made her contribution to the general good by shortening her shooting season and prohibiting the import of dead ducks and geese from abroad during the close season, thereby effectively curtailing the annual massacre of ducks in decoys on the Continent.

5

SHOOTING IN GREAT BRITAIN

FROM the time of the Norman Conquest sporting rights in England have been most jealously preserved and from the earliest days rigid laws concerning the preservation of game have been a feature of the Statute Book. Indeed, it is only little more than a century since the last restrictions of the old laws were abolished and the Game Act of 1831 allowed the ordinary citizen the same sporting rights as his social superiors provided, that he would equip himself with a game licence and could afford to pay for his sport.

The only legal requisite necessary is the annual game license, which can be purchased at any post office from August 1st onwards. Short term licenses are also issued at reduced prices, but the full and usual licence to shoot game costs three pounds. In Ireland, there are rather different rules and scales in the Free State. When provided with a game licence, the sportsman is entitled to own and carry and use smoothbore sporting-guns, but a firearms certificate is necessary in the case of a rifle or a revolver. These certificates are issued by the police on payment of a fee of five shillings, and many arms can be inscribed on one certificate.

The term "game" is a little bit imprecise in English law, but it has been held to cover hares, pheasants, partridges, grouse, blackgame and bustards. It also covers woodcock and snipe; but it is not necessary to own a game licence to shoot ducks, rabbits, wildfowl and pigeons. For these, the possession of a ten-shilling gun licence issued at any post office is all that is required. In general, the visitor would be wiser to buy a game licence, and both this and his firearms certificate, if he is going into a deer forest with a rifle, can be secured for him by his London gunmaker. He is then fully protected and in a sound position, for embarrassing situations occasionally occur to those who have omitted to provide themselves with a full game licence.

The simple possession of these legal papers does not, however, also provide the opportunity to shoot game. All shooting in Great Britain and Northern Ireland is private; the only area where a public right of shooting exists being the sea foreshore between high and low-water marks. This allows a limited amount of wildfowling to coastal communities, but is not worth a visitor's attention as a general rule.

The practice in England is to rent a moor, a deer forest, or a shoot. The outlay for this can be very high, and in practice it is more common for several sportsmen to combine in a syndicate of six or eight guns and share the expenses of the rent, the keeper's wages, the cost of rearing birds, and the general expenses of beaters, luncheon, etc.

In the case of very modest syndicates, what is known as a "rough shoot" is sometimes leased. This carries no full-time keeper and only a small head of game is likely to be found, but it may provide fair sport over dogs.

All game prospects in England and Scotland depend, in so far as grouse and partridges are concerned, largely on the weather and feed conditions during the preceding summer and spring. There is also the possibility of there being no birds because of an epidemic of grouse or partridge disease. In the case of taking a lease of either a moor or a partridge manor the contract should be drawn up by an experienced lawyer and adequate safeguards inserted.

The pheasants in Great Britain are more than nine-tenths specially reared and in a general way these can be depended on. There are, of course, some disaster from epidemics or bad or dishonest keepering, but a mixed shoot with adequate pheasants as well as partridges is probably a far safer investment.

Customarily an advertisement for a gun in a shoot will state the number of acres included in the shoot and the number of pheasants eggs specially put down. A shoot putting down four thousand eggs expects two thousand grown birds from them. The records of previous seasons are kept and a good deal can be learnt from them. Here again, one of the leading London gunmakers would probably be your most useful aid. Syndicates vary in composition: some are close groups of old friends who seldom accept an outside gun without considerable scrutiny. Others are little more than purely business associations and dissolve partnership or seek fresh associations at the end of the season. The best choice of all is a good steady syndicate who for some reason are short of a gun or two at the beginning of the season. Ill-health, business voyages, or anything may cause a vacancy, and in some cases it is convenient for a syndicate to take on an additional gun or a substitute gun for part of the season, a system which meets the needs of a visitor whose stay is limited.

The seasons are in the following sequence. Grouse-shooting begins on August 12th, as does Duck-shooting. Partridge-shooting opens on September 1st and Pheasant-shooting on October 1st. The practical closing dates vary a good deal from the strictly legal ones. Grouse are finished before the end of September, partridges are not shot after Christmas, and not much is left of the pheasants after the New Year. The end of January sees the end of the game season.

The equipment needed in the standard twelve-bore game gun. At large shoots and for grouse or partridge driving a pair of these are needed, the emptied gun being passed back to the loader. In the same way, two large pigskin cartridge bags and two leather cartridge magazines will be needed. At small shoots one gun is enough and one magazine will carry a day's supply. No. 6 shot is almost universal but your gunmaker will advise you on your requirements.

Clothes and boots are important items, for the autumn in Great Britain is a wet season though seldom cold. A good Harris tweed suit, really good waterproof shooting boots, a light but well-proofed raincoat and a telescopic shooting seat represent essentials. The usual American shooting jackets do not appear to be very suitable here, and again, repeating automatic shotguns are an error.

The essential difference between American and British shooting is that in Great Britain nine-tenths of the game is not walked up over dogs but driven by men over a fixed line of

guns. In the case of grouse, the guns are in breast-high "hides" or butts; in partridge-shooting they may line behind a hedgerow, and for pheasant-shooting they may be in a line in the open with forty yards interval between them, facing the woodland or "covert" from which the game will be driven.

There is no limit to the day's bag. A certain number of sections or "beats" are taken, usually six or seven in a day's shooting, and half a dozen guns using a pair of guns apiece may take several hundred birds during the day at a big shoot. At a small, modest single gun shoot, the half-dozen members of the syndicate would probably shoot something between one and two hundred birds between them. Some syndicates shoot once a week for one day, others two successive days alternate weeks. It depends on the size of the ground and the head of game.

There is, it must be admitted, no particular merit in quantity alone, but some stands invariably produce a higher, swifter and more difficult bird than others. It is this combination of difficulty and quantity which is in general most sought after.

Only a small proportion of the game driven over falls to the guns. The remainder stays on the shoot, and is available for later days. If for any reason birds are backward, or have been shot too heavily, the member charged with the running of the shoot calls for a light day, when certain beats are left blank. In this way the supply of game is enough to last the season and afford enough rearing stock for next year.

To the uninitiated this system in its broad outline may seem poor sport and easy. Actually it is considerably more difficult to hit driven birds than those walked up, and a few weeks of actual experience will allay those fears or native convictions which for a time make anyone unaccustomed to strange systems of sport a little critical of them. Judging from the number of eminent American sportsmen who visit us annually, we can show good sport in Great Britain, but it is, owing to the small size of the island, rather more intensively planned than American shooting.

Our labour costs are relatively low, and country men and boys like to earn their pay and the lunch and have a good outing beating. Many of them do it more for the love of a bit of sport than for the reward, and they are pretty good judges of prowess.

There are one or two things which may sound elementary, but yet should be mentioned. In Great Britain you are normally shooting with a line of men advancing towards you. They are invisible and make relatively little noise. The less they make the better, for then the birds flush in small bodies and do not rise in a mob while to become your before you can reload or change guns.

It is, I think, always unwise to shoot ground game—hares, rabbit or roebuck—to your front. Even an experienced English shot cannot tell where beaters are in thick cover, and while a shot after the quarry has passed through the gun line is safe, one in front is seldom so except in special circumstances. A visitor will be all the more respected as a good sportsman if he never takes a chance in front at ground game. Another point is in connection with woodcock, which breed here to a limited extent but arrive in moderate quantity as migrants from October. The woodcock is a night bird and flies with vagary and uncertainty in strong daylight and at about the level of a man's head. Traditionally he is an important trophy, but in practice he is responsible for a lot of accidents. People get excited and forget that they are aiming down the line. Woodcock and low-flying grouse are dangerous creatures. The rest of our feathered game is high enough on the wing to make accident rather improbable, but in a syndicate a good insurance policy against shooting someone else or being shot is not a matter to be disregarded. Your bank manager can manage a "Lloyds" for you. I think I ought to advise this, for while an accidental homicide can be bridged between friends, the modern syndicate is rather less friendly, and you are liable in common law for damages.

The holiday season of the American begins in August, and he has to be back at the tape-machine by mid-September, so few of the younger and keener American shots ever see much except grouse and possibly a few days partridge-driving. It is still quite an open question whether grouse or partridge really afford the finest shooting when shown to their best. It is as unsettleable a problem as that of blondes and brunettes. Pheasant shooting, which is really the mainstay of our island practice, does not begin nominally till October, but actually till the frosts and the autumn rains and winds have cleared the woods of under covert.

By that time most migrant Americans have left, but those who have decided to endure our English winter season in the country (which is, of course, the only part of the year that the country-dwelling English sportsman considers at all endurable) have settled down to it, with the air of cats who have at last discovered the difference between thick cream and separated milk.

Wildfowling I speak about with reluctance. It is, so far as many of our coasts are concerned, more a matter of indifferent literature than any reliable quantity of fowl. It is good in Scotland, and on some estuaries, but our migrant fowl do not come in quantity till there is hard weather on the Baltic. Then, as a rule, it is fairly hard here. It is good sport for the young man with no war wounds and unlimited optimism; but I note that most of the really keen wildfowlers live on the coast, are satisfied with astonishingly inedible trophies, and I am not sure that I consider them better than anglers so far as veracity rather than imagination is concerned. Here we do not to any large extent shoot over decoys or use boats. Our seas are rough and there are happier experiences.

We have, however, called a halt in the wasteful duck slaughter through the International Committee for Bird Protection. I am a member of the English sub-committee on wild-fowl, and our conclusions were that ducks were diminishing, but that sportsmen were not responsible. A few years investigation of facts and rumours saddled the blame pretty squarely on the dead duck industry of Holland. There they decoy the birds into net pipes and wring their necks. With cold storage you can get wild duck all the year round at a restaurant, but you can't get one easily now with a gun on the mud flats.

We were successful in arranging a new law. It allowed duck shooting to begin on the twelfth of August, not the first, and it lopped off an equal amount at the other end of the season, giving in all a month's extra close time. The choice of the date of the twelfth of August was a bit arbitrary but rather democratic. If millionaires should shoot grouse on that date, the poor man (we have hardly any proletarians in England, we are too dignified and sensible) should be allowed his small portion on that date. I do not say it was the best biological date but it was the most statesmanlike date, for it raised no injustices and, of

REDHEADS   RING-NECKED DUCK

CANVAS BACKS

course, in August, all our coast is crowded by charabancs and trippers, and shooting is just hopeless. However, it is quite effective in that it stops flapper-shooting of birds in eclipse plumage, hardly able to fly, and it is going to be implemented by all sportsmen.

There is no market shooting in England now. All the tales of punt guns and the old histories have been knocked out by economics. You could not pay your way for powder and shot on them. The sport remains, and occasionally you can hear the "boom" of a punt gun, but it is not doing any harm. I do not know of any gunmaker who, during the last twenty years has stocked punt-guns. He might have an exhibition piece or so—Bland has—but otherwise he will say "To special order, sir, and I do not like to quote." As the sporting editor of *Country Life*, and as something of an authority on small guns, I do not know of anything new on punt-guns for the last twenty years. They are obsolescent cannon, but they fire a vast deal more shot than ever reaches a duck or the humblest of waders. It is a very technical affair, as intricate as foil fencing, and really belongs to much the same forgotten period.

In my youth, ambition rose to 4-bores and 8-bores, but these ponderous pieces could not be moved swiftly except by men of Herculean physique and unnatural optimism. To-day, if you want to go wildfowling you buy a rather heavy 12-bore for the three-inch long case, and if you can stand knee high in cold mud and shoot, with good fortune you may get some duck and sea geese. Well, we all of us feel the call of the wild, but I can't honestly advise it as a sport for the visitor. He may perhaps prefer it because of its miseries and privations, but I believe it is so much better in countries far nearer the United States. I have had such incredible duck-shooting in Mexico that I have never dared say a word about it. In Spain I can get the same thing, but in Great Britain I cannot honestly recommend it unless you have a highborn sporting friend with a good place and no delusions.

If I see three wildfowlers with a dozen birds between them and three of these worth cooking, I know they have had a good day. But then, in this country teeming with game, the average wildfowler is a man who can't afford a shoot.

We shall get the thing straightened out in about a decade, for we are in Great Britain all conscious that in order to get good shooting and preserve it for future generations, we have to put back what we take.

We have practised it for over a century and only in this twentieth century did it dawn upon the greedy that you can't grow ten birds to the acre when nature limits it to a pair. Over production of game just sheer greed—introduced partridge disease, a form of strongylosis. It swept the over-populated partridge manors and was as bad as grouse disease. But common biological sense is the last thing an estate owner wants to hear when he has banked on plain unnatural sin and an inflated "game market."

We do not know yet a great deal about bird diseases: most of them are epizootic, which is scientific jargon for "epidemic" as we know the word. We do not know with any approach to quantitative values what birds eat or how the things they eat affect them. One type of country will carry an enormous head of game and another will not.

In order to work out why these diseases exist you have to know about a dozen different sciences and to be able to use your brain. Most of the former concepts of nutrition have been upset by the discovery of accessory food factors such as vitamins. A great deal is now known about these so far as human nutrition goes, but if a horse grabs a mouthful of green-stuff by the roadside we have no real knowledge of what the plug is really putting into his system.

It is the same with birds. We do not know what they eat and we don't know the effect of the things they eat. It has been a hobby of mine to sit up with scalpel and microscope and try to get some idea of it. I have been through the phases of belief which have marked most advances in the science of nutrition during the last twenty years. And I still do not know what an old cock pheasant walking across my land or paddock eats in the way of herbs. One thing I am perfectly certain about: he eats things whose effect is still not known to science.

We all know that acorns are good for hogs, but few people realize that they are mainly a vermifuge. It is the same way with birds. An acid herb such as sorrel may oblige the coccidia in a pheasant's intestine to evacuate, that is, put on their shell overcoats and get out. It is that matter of cause and effect which is what we must know before we really know what we are doing.

I remember an admirable biological survey of the Bob White Quail, and the one sentence which shocked me was that "they had not got a compound microscope." This was just like trying out a frontal attack on a position held by modern machine-guns armed with pikes and halberds.

I do not specify the work. It was excellent, but to be starved of microscopes, the working tools, that seemed to me to show that whoever administered the funds ought to have been sweeping crossings. But perhaps this is unfair, for a microscope, like a gun, is a real instrument in some hands and a complete washout in others. Ninety per cent of people only see what they have been taught to believe will be there. The remaining ten per cent see something more, and out of that comes original thought, like Pasteur's.

I think that the field of ecology for game preservation and conservation is enormous, but I think that we need a great deal more original work and observation not based on printed stuff. There is an enormous fund of material in the "rule of thumb." Old English gamekeepers will give tea made of willow leaves to birds with "gapes." It works, and they get rid of the gape worm. In effect, they have been given "salicin," and modern science will not contest with you that there is a better line of attack.

I am certain that the United States, with its wide variation of climatic conditions, can become a game reserve where birds little known outside zoological collections to-day can become natural game. Experiment must follow on experiment, but after all there is no nation in the world so open to progressive ideas as the United States. But these biological matters are not easy. All who are keen and interested have to learn, and then to unlearn, every idea. Science is, after all, only what we believe to be true at the moment. It progresses, and old ideas are left as shells.

I think that with the modern idea of really understanding nature in its surroundings we are advancing to a point where it will be possible for man to put back what he takes out and maintain a balance, not perhaps of nature, for while man develops the earth that is impossible, but a balance adequate for the sportsman.

Our English systems are not without fault, but they are very fairly efficient. They represent about a century and a half of logical progress towards the maintenance of a head of game in these islands, and as to its success, I cannot say more than that the average bag is about 500 per cent better than it was a century ago, so far as game is concerned. So far as wild fowl is concerned, we have not overshot, but the rest of Europe has.

Salvation comes from a better and far more scientific understanding of the problems affecting game. The ordinary "scientific worker" may or may not be useful. He has his qualifications, but these are of little account. The only man worth counting from the sportsman's point of view is the scientist with a real appreciation of the unexplored problem. Well, they will turn up, usually unpopular, but among a million or so zoologists we have had only one, Sir Arthur Shipley, who ran the Grouse Commission and wrote the first and still the unsurpassed guide to scientific inquiry on game birds.

Neither degrees nor qualifications nor influence can really serve. The combination of scientist and sportsman is rare. In England we are mostly amateurs, with possibly a spoof degree *Honoris Causa* tucked away for other services to the State.

We have got public opinion and support behind us now on both hemispheres, and we can maintain a head of game. I am frankly an optimist, but I know that under suitable conditions aviculturalists have been able to preserve in England and Europe species nearly extinct in their native habitats. It is our task, in the newer conception, to make these species common. Some of them should never be shot in our time, but there is no reason why they should not provide sport for our descendants.

Every sportsman in the world wants good fair sport, and it is only by conservation and international action that we can get it. So far as I know, the Germans and the Italians have behaved well and have been not only sensible but practical. It is, I must admit, a pretty crazy European world, but it is quite possible that the odd concept which we know as sportsmanship may yet prove an ethical factor.

Actually nothing is better for nature than a human war. When things were simply awful in Spain under the Republic everyone came out and stole eggs and killed nesting birds, but the war has done a lot of good. It stopped all that, and the bird reserves of Spain are now one of the best hopes for the western seaboard of Europe. Ducks fly down the two peninsulas of Italy and Spain. And Spain has now, under General Franco and in the person of the Marques del Merito, joined the International Committee for the Protection of Bird Life, and completes the whole of the civilized seaboard nations of Europe.

SHOOTING IN AMERICA

THE fundamentals of actual field shooting in America are quite similar to those in England, but the conditions under which the sport is practised here are very different from those in England.

When the colonists arrived here, the struggle for existence left little room for sport in the important process of killing game for food. The game was free to all who could take it, except in those few instances where the Crown gave grants (some of which are still in existence) which included the rights of fishing, fowling and oystering. Such rights were ceded to the Smith family on Long Island, and to-day the town of Brookhaven controls the wildfowling and oystering rights in Bellport Bay, these rights having been transferred to the town by the Smith family. I mention this instance, because it is almost unique in America.

Generally speaking, all non-migratory fish and game belongs to the State in which it is found. A Fish and Game Commission, often made up of men who serve without pay, is in charge of this asset of their State. It is they who oversee the operation of the State fish hatcheries and game farms, and the distribution of the fish and game raised; and they organize and maintain a body of game and fish wardens who uphold the State laws governing fishing and shooting.

The work of such fish and game commissions is supported by the funds derived from the sale of State fishing and hunting licences. I might say here that in America the use of the term "hunting" is not confined to foxhunting; in fact, the average citizen will use "hunting" to mean shooting, and the shooting licence will be entitled "Hunting Licence."

The cost of a licence to a resident of a State will average in the neighbourhood of three dollars; a non-resident licence for fishing will cost about five dollars, and one for hunting from ten to twenty dollars, according to the State and the game to be sought for.

It must be understood that unless a property owner "posts" his land with signs forbidding shooting and fishing and trespassing, the public is entitled to enter upon it for the purpose of shooting and fishing. In some States, if an owner permits the commission to stock his waters or land with fish or game, it then becomes unlawful for the owner to post his property to prevent the public from seeking this State fish and game.

In the case of migratory game, the Federal Government exercises general control, based, in the case of wildfowl, upon a treaty we have with Canada. A "Duck Stamp" which may be purchased at any post office for a dollar, must be affixed to the wildfowler's regular state hunting licence, and the revenue thus produced is used by the Biological Survey—the bureau of the Federal Government in charge of fish and game—to protect the migratory

43

birds. The Biological Survey actually dictates the open seasons on all migratory game birds, and the States generally change their laws to conform with the Federal law. There is a small force of Federal game wardens active in enforcing these Federal laws.

Before planning a shooting trip in the States, an Englishman should definitely ascertain from the Fish and Game Commission of any State in which he purposes to shoot whether a shooting licence may be issued to an alien in that State. Several States attach certain conditions to the purchase of shooting and fishing licences by aliens, due to their large and (in the sporting sense) undesirable foreign populations. A list of the proper names and addresses of all State Fish and Game Commissions may be obtained from the Biological Survey, Washington, D.C.

In addition to the open shooting in America, one finds a number of private plantations and clubs, where the best shooting is to be had. Correspondence with an American sporting friend would be the most practical way in which to get reliable information on this subject.

Let us now consider the shooting afforded by some of the more important game birds in America.

UPLAND BIRDS

The bob white quail is probably the most popular game bird in this country. He is found fairly well scattered over the entire eastern half of the United States, and heavily concentrated in the southern part.

The finest quail shooting is found in North and South Carolina, Tennessee, Arkansas, Georgia, Florida, Alabama, Mississippi and Texas. On many of the large plantations and clubs, one follows on horseback a pair of fast, wide-ranging pointers, dismounting for the shot when the dogs point a bevy of birds. Quail flush as one bird and fly with very considerable speed, usually heading for the nearest thick cover, where they drop scattered, later to reassemble into a bevy when danger is past. As the bevies are generally found while feeding in the open fields, they fly fairly low and straight until they reach cover. Quail are fast on the wing. After the bevy shot, one follows up the singles and enjoys what most sportsmen consider the best part of quail shooting.

As the weather is usually quite warm, pointers have been found more suitable than setters in the Southern quail country. Often the sportsman and his guide are followed by a light wagon on which there is a crate containing an extra brace of dogs. On hot days each brace is hunted for about an hour at a time. The country is so large that untired and fast dogs add much to the sportsman's pleasure as well as to the size of his bag, which, generally speaking, is limited to fifteen birds a day.

Due to the fact that the birds do not leave the woods to feed until around nine o'clock in the morning, one gains little by going out very early. By five in the afternoon they are leaving the open, and at sundown they take wing, never walking, to their roosting-place in the fields bordering some thick cover. The bevy roosts in a small circle, each bird facing out from the centre, so that if disturbed they can take wing in all directions at once. From the roost they retire to the woods early in the morning, later returning to the open to feed.

It is necessary to buy a shooting licence, in some instances from the State, which entitles one to shoot anywhere within its limits, and in other instances from the county; but it is never necessary to buy both. This is a matter of local law. No. 9 shot is customarily used for quail.

In the northern part of the United States is found what we generally consider the finest of all game birds, the ruffed grouse. This wily and strong-flying bird is usually shot over a close-working, careful and experienced setter or pointer. Sometimes a grouse hunter will walk up his birds, with a spaniel at heel for retrieving. These birds are found in the mountains, and the going is often very difficult, what with climbing hardwood ridges and working through rhododendron and alder swamps.

When a grouse is flushed, it is with a burst of speed that puts the bird in full flight almost immediately. The roar of wings is very startling in the still autumn air, and a beginner is quite likely to forget to shoot until it is too late. One has to see to believe the skill with which a grouse will place a tree or rock between himself and the gunner. The successful grouse hunter must be an unusually fast shot, with nerves keyed up to a high pitch all the while he is in good coverts.

Grouse are found either singly or in coveys of from four to six; but all the members of a covey do not flush simultaneously as do quail. The importance of having a very steady and experienced dog is most obvious when a covey is found. First one bird roars out of the thicket, flying with terrific speed through the trees. One takes a snap shot, perhaps aiming at a spot several feet ahead of where the bird has disappeared behind a hemlock tree; and a good shot will kill a remarkably high number of times after the bird has actually passed out of sight. If the dog is not steady to shot, he will have flushed more birds; but if he knows his job, he will be standing like a statue. Without any warning a second bird flushes, and before the gun is up another drives off at full speed in the opposite direction.

Grouse carry shot in a most discouraging manner, and while the average man uses No. 7½ shot, I have found that the increased number of pellets afforded by No. 9's is more likely to break a wing, which drives the bird down far quicker than a body-hit with heavier shot. Success in ruffed-grouse shooting seldom comes to the novice—though he may be a fine shot—while the thoroughly experienced man will make amazingly good bags. Records kept over a number of years show that one bird for six shots is *excellent* shooting.

The woodcock is seldom seen west of the Mississippi, and is not highly esteemed in the South. But in New England and the Middle Atlantic States this lovely little bird is the choice of a comparatively small number of enthusiasts, among which the writer is numbered. One must have a good dog—setter, pointer or spaniel—as the bird lies exceedingly close. The first few days of the open season are usually spent with local birds, but soon these are replaced by flight birds from farther north.

I have been astonished at the number of farmers whose land contains suitable woodcock coverts, who have never seen one of these shy and mysterious creatures. Their flights and most of their feeding take place at night; during the daytime they lie up in alders and other thick cover, seldom moving about until evening.

It is noticeable how many dogs dislike to retrieve woodcock, although I have never seen one that would not hunt them eagerly once he had had a bird shot over him. No. 9

or No. 10 shot is quite sufficient for these tender birds, a single pellet bringing them down. In fact, there have been many instances noted by myself and my friends, when a woodcock has fallen before the gun with absolutely no sign of having a shot in him. Could it be that a wad has hit him, or did he die from the concussion? This sounds far-fetched, but almost every experienced woodcock shot will bear me out.

The flight birds are found on birch-covered hillsides and in alder swamps. When flushed they seldom fly more than sixty yards. As they almost never lie in the open, their initial flight is generally upwards to the top of the cover, and one who is inclined to over-shoot most birds will do well on woodcock.

The open season is for thirty days, the opening dates varying from October 1st in the north to November 15th further south. A State shooting licence is required. In some States, a special woodcock licence must also be had.

The pheasant is now found in suitable types of country clear across the continent. Here we hunt him over dogs, and pretty tame sport it is to shoot pheasant over a setter or pointer. Of late years much better sport has been had with a springer spaniel. Aside from a very few instances, we do not drive the birds as is done in England, although this form of pheasant shooting will probably increase as time goes on.

The bird is so easily raised in captivity that it is widely stocked by the State game authorities. In most States only the cocks may be shot, the hens being carefully protected. The number of farms which raise pheasants and permit shooting over their well-stocked coverts is increasing each year. One pays so much for every bird shot, and the open season for such shooting lasts several months longer than the regular State season. These game farms afford shooting, therefore, at a time when all other seasons are closed, and appear to be gaining steadily in popularity.

At times one has excellent snipe shooting in certain favourable localities—notably Florida. In the northern part of the country, it is generally a matter of happening on a flight of migratory birds, a happy occasion which has not come my way in several years. The shooting is almost identical with that in England and Ireland.

WILDFOWL

Wildfowling in America has been at a low ebb during the past few years. Destruction of nesting areas, over-shooting and other unfavourable elements reduced our stock of wildfowl to such an alarming degree that exceedingly stringent regulatory measures were enforced by the Federal Government in order to prevent what at one time looked like the beginning of the end.

Fortunately these regulations—while they virtually ruined the shooting—did prove sufficiently successful to turn the tide, and it is now agreed that a material increase in the numbers of wildfowl has taken place. Consequently, the restrictions are gradually being lightened, and it is hoped that within a few years really good shooting will be had once more.

Duck shooting has been carried on in roughly three ways in the past: blind shooting over wooden and live decoys; battery shooting out on the feeding grounds of the

deep-water fowl, such as canvas-back, red head and scaup; and walk-up shooting in the swamps and around pond holes and streams.

Blind shooting may be done either from a suitable hide along the salt-water bays and marshes, or on inland waters. Perhaps two dozen wooden decoys are anchored within gunshot of the blind, with one or more live call ducks on the shore. The customary form of hide along salt water is the duck boat, the decks of which are thatched with grass, and with perhaps a bit of grass stuck up around the gunwale of the cockpit. The punties are quite shallow and are pulled up on the shore, preferably in the sedge or marsh grass. Wooden and cork decoys have been developed to an amazing degree, and the older hand-made specimens along tidewater comprise a very interesting form of waterfront sculpture. Some of the old decoy-makers have produced exquisite examples of handiwork. An artificial duck call is often used to lure the birds over the decoys.

Along the Mississippi bottomlands, superb duck shooting has been had in the flooded woods—long-range shooting over the treetops as the birds are called to the gunner. In many shallow lakes which offer excellent feeding grounds, permanent blinds are erected along the shore, or even out in the water.

Baiting the bottom with corn in the vicinity of blinds proved to be a most successful method of producing good shooting—so successful that the government has made it illegal. The use of live decoys has also been forbidden. The open seasons have been drastically reduced.

Battery shooting has likewise been proscribed. A battery is a water-tight box, just large enough for two men to lie in, with decks several feet wide. To the edges of these decks, wings of wood, or canvas on frames, are hinged, to rise and fall with the waves. A strip of soft lead some four to six inches wide, and fastened around the edge of the box, can be bent up to prevent water from slopping into the box in rough weather. A number of solid iron decoys are placed on the deck in order to sink the box to the proper level. In really bad weather a battery cannot be used. The "machine" is painted dull water grey in colour, and the gunners' clothes are of a similar colour. From two hundred to four hundred wooden decoys are set out around, and mostly to leeward of the anchored battery. The deep-water ducks, which spend their time in the open bays, decoy very satisfactorily to such a rig, and enormous bags have been made in the past.

A tender is required to serve the battery. When a bird has been crippled, the gunner of course attempts to kill it; but if he fails, he makes a certain signal with his arm, and the tender attempts to secure the bird. If birds are killed, another signal is given, and the tender picks up the game as quickly as possible and retires to his position some half a mile away, where he anchors and awaits the next call.

Walk-up shooting is done in much the same manner as in England, a retriever often being used.

Retrievers are more and more being employed in blind shooting, and I feel that the Chesapeake Bay dog is the ideal breed for our purposes. He has been bred to a dead grass colour, and lying quietly in or beside the blind, does not interfere in the least with decoying birds. His strength and endurance are remarkable, and he will time and time again swim out among floating ice to retrieve his birds—and obviously enjoy the work. Incidentally, the Chesapeake is one of the two purely American breeds of dogs, the other being the Boston Bull.

When one looks back on the days of professional market-gunning, when every hotel and restaurant of any pretensions was serving wildfowl, one must be thrilled at the vast myriads of ducks which then migrated over this country. The early settlers killed wildfowl in count- less millions for their own use. Professional guides had thousands of decoys, several batteries and perhaps a dozen punties, in one outfit for sportsmen clients. Duck shooting was a thriving business along the sea-coasts and such flyways as the Mississippi Valley. The perfection of our gunning methods reached such a point that the wildfowl of America were well on their way to extinction. With the terrible example of the passenger pigeon and the bison before us, we have come to realize that the strictest regulation must be practised to save our wildfowl, and it is not too early to predict that the situation is in hand. Never again will a single battery account for over five hundred birds in one day. Never again will blinds make bags of a hundred ducks in a day. But the vast army of wildfowlers which follow the sport in this country will, I am confident, be able to take five to ten birds apiece a day for many years to come, under the regulations which will be in force.

Co-operation with the government and sportsmen of Canada is already restoring breeding grounds in that country, for it is Canada which is now the great wildfowl nursery of this continent.